Cases and Materials on Business Entities
2007-2008 Supplement

ASPEN PUBLISHERS

Cases and Materials on Business Entities

2007-2008 Supplement

Eric A. Chiappinelli

Associate Dean for Alumni and Professional Relations
Professor of Law
Seattle University School of Law

www.BusinessEntitiesOnline.com

Wolters Kluwer
Law & Business

AUSTIN   BOSTON   CHICAGO   NEW YORK   THE NETHERLANDS

Aspen Publishers
Attn: Permissions Department
76 Ninth Avenue, 7th Floor
New York, NY 10011-5201

To contact Customer Care, e-mail customer.care@aspenpublishers.com,
call 1-800-234-1660, fax 1-800-901-9075, or mail correspondence to:

Aspen Publishers
Attn: Order Department
PO Box 990
Frederick, MD 21705

Printed in the United States of America.

1 2 3 4 5 6 7 8 9 0

ISBN 978-0-7355-7015-3

Library of Congress Cataloging-in-Publication Data

Chiappinelli, Eric A., 1953-
    Cases and materials on business entities / Eric A. Chiappinelli.
        p. cm.
    ISBN 0-7355-2614-1 (casebound)
    ISBN 978-0-7355-7015-3 (supplement)
        1.   Corporation law – United states – Cases. 2. Business enterprises – Law
        and Legislation – United States – Cases. I. title.
KF1413.C485 2006
346.73'066 – dc22   2006003929

About Wolters Kluwer Law & Business

Wolters Kluwer Law & Business is a leading provider of research information and workflow solutions in key specialty areas. The strengths of the individual brands of Aspen Publishers, CCH, Kluwer Law International and Loislaw are aligned within Wolters Kluwer Law & Business to provide comprehensive, in-depth solutions and expert-authored content for the legal, professional and education markets.

CCH was founded in 1913 and has served more than four generations of business professionals and their clients. The CCH products in the Wolters Kluwer Law & Business group are highly regarded electronic and print resources for legal, securities, antitrust and trade regulation, government contracting, banking, pension, payroll, employment and labor, and healthcare reimbursement and compliance professionals.

Aspen Publishers is a leading information provider for attorneys, business professionals and law students. Written by preeminent authorities, Aspen products offer analytical and practical information in a range of specialty practice areas from securities law and intellectual property to mergers and acquisitions and pension/benefits. Aspen's trusted legal education resources provide professors and students with high-quality, up-to-date and effective resources for successful instruction and study in all areas of the law.

Kluwer Law International supplies the global business community with comprehensive English-language international legal information. Legal practitioners, corporate counsel and business executives around the world rely on the Kluwer Law International journals, loose-leafs, books and electronic products for authoritative information in many areas of international legal practice.

Loislaw is a premier provider of digitized legal content to small law firm practitioners of various specializations. Loislaw provides attorneys with the ability to quickly and efficiently find the necessary legal information they need, when and where they need it, by facilitating access to primary law as well as state-specific law, records, forms and treatises.

Wolters Kluwer Law & Business, a unit of Wolters Kluwer, is headquartered in New York and Riverwoods, Illinois. Wolters Kluwer is a leading multinational publisher and information services company.

Table of Contents

Preface

The purpose of this Preface is to tell you, whether you're a professor or a student, what you can expect in this Supplement. There are six kinds of materials here. First are recent, important developments in caselaw. The Delaware courts in particular have been quite busy since January 2006, when the text of the casebook was finalized. Second are recent cases of less importance but that make pedagogically useful additions to the text. Third are recent cases that are meant to replace cases in the casebook, either because the casebook case is older or because it doesn't teach as well as the case here. Fourth are casebook errata that make a difference in comprehension. That is to say, I've put corrections here for things in the casebook that were just plain wrong when I wrote them. I think there are mercifully few of these. Fifth are statutory changes since the book was written. Both the MBCA and the DGCL have made a few changes of importance to corporate law professors—at least those corporate law professors using this casebook. Sixth are discussions of two substantive areas of great current interest. One is the options backdating scandal, which is considered both doctrinally in Chapter 11, and more generally in Chapter 14. The other is the simple majority vote movement, which is covered in Chapter 15.

I describe each of the important developments in this Supplement to let you know why it's here. As with the casebook itself, my criteria for selection are recent cases (less than 20 years old, with few exceptions) that present issues suitable for upper division law students in an introductory course in business entities, and that seem to me to be teachable.

As in the casebook, following each case are Notes and Questions. One of the most useful features of this casebook is the way in which the Notes and Questions sections are organized. I have divided the notes and questions into five types, labeled each, and set them out in the same order throughout the book. Not every Notes and Questions section will have each type. The first type is called, believe it or not, Notes. This has factual information, usually about the preceding case, the kind of transaction, or the applicable law. The second type is called Reality Check. These questions are designed to make sure you understand the transaction, the dispute, and the resolution. They should be of particular value before class and at the end of the course, when you're preparing for the final exam. The third type is called Suppose. These questions ask you to be a bit flexible in your thinking. They ask you to imagine that the facts or the law were slightly different from the actual case. One of a lawyer's most frequent tasks is to analogize or distinguish one set of facts from another. The Suppose questions give you practice in doing that. The fourth type is called What Do You Think? These are policy and theory questions. They ask you for your view of the case's result on the parties, the social effect of the rule in the case, or a more general theoretical question. These may seem a bit divorced from reality at first, but I think law students tend to underestimate the power of theory on the world in which they live.

Finally, some of the Notes and Questions sections end with a You Draft It exercise. These are, as you see by the name, opportunities to hone your drafting skills. My pedagogical view is that drafting exercises that are simply made up by the professor are not nearly as valuable as those drawn from actual legal practice. Moreover, I believe that an underappreciated writing skill is the talent to draft small, very focused, pieces. Every You Draft It assignment is based on actual language that was important in the case just discussed.

Highlights of the Contents

If you teach nothing else from this Supplement, you should cover the following:

Stone v. Ritter in Chapter 11
This reconceptualizes *Caremark* and deals with the duty of good faith.

Desimone v. Barrows in Chapter 11
This case discusses the corporate law issues involved in backdating options.

ATR-Kim Eng Financial Corp. v. Araneta in Chapter 13
This is important because it's a thoughtful application of *Caremark* and holds directors liable for breaching *Caremark* duties.

The Backdated Options Scandal in Chapter 14
The text summarizes the corporate responsibility aspects of the backdating scandal in light of the post-Enron reforms.

The Simple Majority Vote Movement in Chapter 15
The rise of this important shareholder activist initiative and the statutory implications are discussed here.

Seinfeld v. Verizon Communications, Inc. in Chapter 15
This case is important, although it reaffirmed the long-standing rule, because it suggests that the Delaware courts may focus their attention on shareholder books and records rights.

Finally, I want to point out that www.BusinessEntitiesOnline.com provides both students and professors with additional resources, including new case developments.

Acknowledgments

Maremont, Mark and Charles Forelle. *Bosses' Pay: How Stock Options Became Part of the Problem*. The Wall Street Journal, December 27, 2006, at A1. Reprinted with permission of Dow Jones & Company, Inc., conveyed through Copyright Clearance Center, Inc.

Murray, Alan. *Will Backdating Scandal Thwart Effort to Roll Back Reforms?* The Wall Street Journal, December 20, 2006, at A2. Reprinted with permission of Dow Jones & Company, Inc., conveyed through Copyright Clearance Center, Inc.

White, Erin. *Stage-Managing the Annual Meeting*. The Wall Street Journal, April 16, 2007, at B1. Reprinted with permission of Dow Jones & Company, Inc., conveyed through Copyright Clearance Center, Inc.

Cases and Materials on Business Entities
2007-2008 Supplement

Chapter 4
Agency

Page 96

Replace *In the Matter of McDuffie* with:

Udall v. T.D. Escrow Services, Inc.
154 P.3d 882 (Wash. 2007)

FAIRHURST, J.

William Udall purchased real property in a nonjudicial foreclosure sale. The auctioneer gave Udall a receipt, but not the deed of trust for the property. When trustee T.D. Escrow Services, Inc. (hereinafter T.D.) discovered that the auctioneer had opened the bidding $100,000 lower than T.D. had authorized, T.D. refused to deliver the deed to Udall. We reverse the Court of Appeals and reinstate the trial court's summary judgment ruling quieting title in Udall.

FACTUAL AND PROCEDURAL HISTORY

The material facts are undisputed. After the borrowers defaulted on their home mortgage payments, lender U.S. Bancorp directed T.D. to commence nonjudicial foreclosure proceedings on the property. T.D. properly recorded a notice of trustee's sale announcing that it would "sell [the property] at public auction to the highest and best bidder" "as provided by statute" to satisfy the "obligation secured by the Deed of Trust."

T.D. employs ABC Legal Services (hereinafter ABC) to conduct Washington-based nonjudicial foreclosure sales. On the morning of April 16, 2004, T.D. communicated to ABC by telephone the opening bids for that day's sales, identifying the opening bid for the property as $159,421.20. At the auction, ABC auctioneer Donna Hayes distributed to attendees an information sheet listing properties being sold that day and opening bids. The opening bid listed for the property was $59,421.20.

Hayes read the standardized nonjudicial foreclosure sale script and announced the opening bid of $59,421.20. Udall bid one dollar more. There being no other bidders, Hayes closed the sale. Udall tendered full payment and

Hayes gave Udall a receipt for the property. Consistent with T.D.'s policy, the deed of trust for the property was not issued to Udall at the sale.[1]

T.D. discovered the discrepancy in the opening bid when Udall's funds were transmitted to its main office. In a letter dated April 21, 2004, T.D. returned to Udall a check for the amount he had paid for the property and explained that ABC had not been authorized to open bidding at $59,421.20. Udall rejected the refund. T.D. refused to issue the deed of trust to Udall.

Udall brought an action to quiet title, naming T.D. and lender U.S. Bancorp as defendants. The trial court granted summary judgment quieting title in Udall. The Court of Appeals Division Two reversed the ruling and entered summary judgment in favor of T.D.

ANALYSIS

The Court of Appeals held that T.D. did not have a duty to deliver the deed to Udall because "ABC lacked actual or apparent authority to sell the property for $59,422.20 [and] to accept a bid for this amount." We disagree with the conclusion that ABC did not have apparent authority to sell the property to Udall.

An agent has apparent authority when a third party reasonably believes the agent has authority to act on behalf of the principal and that belief is traceable to the principal's manifestations. RESTATEMENT (THIRD) OF AGENCY § 2.03, at 113 (2006). Apparent authority may exist in agents who act beyond the scope of their actual authority.[5]

The court's focus on ABC's needing apparent authority "to sell the property *at the mistakenly low opening price*," or any particular price, is misplaced. The appropriate analysis focuses on whether Udall believed, based on T.D.'s manifestations, that ABC had "authority to act for" T.D. to sell the property on T.D.'s behalf, and whether that belief was "objectively reasonable." A principal may "make a manifestation by ... placing an agent in charge of a transaction or situation." RESTATEMENT, *supra,* § 3.03 cmt. b at 174. T.D., by issuing the notice of trustee's sale, made just such a manifestation.[6] Based on T.D.'s representation, Udall could reasonably believe that T.D. or its authorized agent would conduct the sale. When ABC auctioneer Hayes in fact conducted

---

[1] It is T.D.'s policy before issuing a deed of trust to verify the validity of a bid and receipt of funds, as well as to check for intervening bankruptcies and other potential problems that might affect the sale.

[5] It is undisputed that T.D. directed ABC to open bidding on the property at $159,421.20. As a result, ABC lacked actual authority to open bidding on the property at $59,421.20.

[6] The notice announced "NOTICE IS HEREBY GIVEN THAT the undersigned Trustee, [T.D.], will ... sell at public auction to the highest and best bidder, payable at the time of the sale, the [property]."

the sale, Udall was reasonable in believing that she did so as T.D.'s authorized agent.

T.D. employed ABC to conduct its nonjudicial foreclosure sales in Washington. At this sale, Hayes read the standard script and announced the opening bid as $59,421.20. It is undisputed that the opening bid was erroneous, but the error did not create a duty in Udall, an arm's length third party, to question whether the announced bid was the amount authorized by T.D.

T.D.'s manifestations provided Udall with an objectively reasonable basis to conclude that ABC, through Hayes, had authority to act for T.D. in conducting the property sale. Hayes thus acted with apparent authority when she accepted Udall's high bid and closed the sale. Principal T.D. was bound by that acceptance. T.D. must deliver the deed of trust to Udall.

Grossly inadequate purchase price together with circumstances indicating some additional unfairness may provide sufficient equitable grounds to set aside a nonjudicial foreclosure sale.

In this case, T.D. made no showing that unfairness prejudiced the borrower, and the price, more than 35 percent of the intended opening bid, cannot be deemed grossly inadequate. We decline to invalidate this nonjudicial foreclosure sale where no grounds for equitable intervention are present.

CONCLUSION

We reverse the Court of Appeals and reinstate the trial court's award of summary judgment quieting title in Udall.

Notes and Questions

1. Notes

a. The Washington Court of Appeals found the following additional facts:

> Nor does the record show that ABC had apparent authority to sell the property at the mistakenly low opening price that Udall bid and ABC "accepted." The only arguable communication between Udall and TD was indirect, through TD's September 19, 2003 Notice of Trustee's Sale; this Notice stated that the property owner owed the lender $148,031.24, and the property would be priced higher than $148,000 in order to satisfy the existing debt. This Notice of Trustee's Sale did not establish that auctioneer ABC had apparent authority to open bidding at $59,421.20 or any other price lower than that necessary to satisfy seller Brown's [the homeowner] debt on the property.

The record contains no other arguable communication between TD and Udall, direct or indirect. Thus, Udall cannot satisfy the requirement that, to establish "apparent authority," the principal (TD) must have manifested to the third party (Udall) that the agent (ABC) had *apparent* authority to act on its behalf. Here, there was no such communication that Udall could have reasonably and objectively interpreted as creating such apparent authority in ABC.[5]

Udall v. T.D. Escrow Services, Inc., 130 P.3d 908, 913 (Wash. App. 2006).

2. Reality Check

a. What was Ms. Hayes' actual authority? What was her apparent authority?

b. In what way did T.D. create apparent authority in Ms. Hayes?

3. Suppose

a. Suppose Ms. Hayes had opened the bidding at $15,942.12. If Mr. Udall had bid one dollar more, would the court have reached the same result?

b. Suppose Ms. Hayes had opened the bidding at $1,594.21. If Mr. Udall had bid one dollar more, would the court have reached the same result?

4. What Do You Think?

a. If agency is a consensual relationship, how can the principal be held to an action by its agent to which it did not consent?

b. Do you think the Supreme Court was correct or was the Court of Appeals correct? Why?

---

[5] In our view, ABC's mere appearance at the auction and pronouncement of the mistakenly low opening bid does not meet the Act's requirement for a communication between TD and Udall establishing a reasonable belief that ABC had apparent authority to sell the property at this price. Further detracting from Udall's claim of apparent authority was his vast experience as a sophisticated, foreclosure-sale purchaser who has purchased 100 foreclosed properties since 1995. Such an experienced foreclosure-sale purchaser should have had actual knowledge of ABC's lack of actual or apparent authority to sell the property at the auctioneer's opening bid price because this bid was $90,000 lower than the known amount the foreclosure sale had to yield to satisfy the property owner's debt.

c. Should Mr. Udall have to show some reliance on Ms. Hayes' action or some potential harm from allowing T.D. to reject his bid in order to prevail? Could Mr. Udall have made such a showing?

Page 99

Add the following case before "**c. Principal's Liability to Third Parties for Actions Actually or Apparently Authorized**":

If you or your client is dealing with a business entity, that entity must obviously act through humans. How will you or your client know whether those humans are authorized to act on behalf of the entity? If those people act outside their actual authority, can you hold the entity liable under the theory of apparent authority on the basis of the agent's own assertions? Does apparent authority arise from the entity providing the agent a business card with his or her name and title? Does it arise from providing the agent an email account? The next case deals with this very common situation.

CSX Transp., Inc. v. Recovery Express, Inc.
415 F. Supp. 2d 6 (D. Mass. 2006)

YOUNG, District Judge.

I. INTRODUCTION

This is a breach of contract and related equitable action brought by the plaintiff, CSX Transportation, Inc. ("CSX"), against the defendants, Recovery Express, Inc. ("Recovery") and Interstate Demolition and Environmental Corp. ("IDEC"). The case against Recovery turns on the application of that doctrine within the law of agency known as "apparent authority"; specifically, how large a cloak of such authority is provided by access to an e-mail address with a defendant's domain name.

A. Undisputed Facts

CSX is in the business of selling out-of-service railcars and parts. It is a Virginia corporation with its principal place of business in Florida. Recovery is a Massachusetts corporation with its principal place of business in Boston. IDEC was a Delaware corporation with its principal place of business at the same address in Boston. It is now defunct. At all relevant times, IDEC and Recovery shared offices in Boston.

On August 22, 2003, Albert Arillotta ("Arillotta"), a "partner" at IDEC, sent an e-mail to Len Whitehead, Jr. ("Whitehead") of CSX expressing interest in buying "rail cars as scrap" ("the E-mail"). Arillotta represented himself to be "from interstate demolition and recovery express". The e-mail address from which Arillotta sent this inquiry was "albert@recoveryexpress.com". The entire e-mail–horrendous grammar and all–is reproduced here:

> From: Albert Arillotta [albert@recoveryexpress.com]
> Sent: Friday, August 22, 2003 4:57 PM
> To: Whitehead, Len Jr.
> Subject: purchase of out service railcars
>
> lynn this is albert arillotta from interstate demolition and recovery express we are interested in buying rail cars for scrap paying you a percentage of what the amm maket indicator is there are several locations i suggest to work at the exsisting location of the rail cars. we will send you a brochure and financials per your request our address is the following:
> interstate demolition/recoveryexpress
> 180 canal street 5th floor boston mass 02114
> phone number 617-523-7740
> fax number 617-367-3627
> email address albert @recoveryexpress.com
>
> thank you for your time

There apparently were subsequent phone calls between Whitehead and Arillotta, Decl. of Len Whitehead, Jr., but the substance of the calls is not recounted. CSX alleges that it prepared and forwarded sales order forms which "confirm[ed] the agreed[-]upon terms [of the sale] to IDEC." Neither CSX nor Recovery has provided copies of these forms. Apparently, Arillotta and Whitehead proceeded with this proposed deal.

The railcars were "delivered ... to the location specified by Arillotta ...." Recovery claims that this location was, in fact, CSX's own railyard, to which Arillotta went himself, disassembled the cars, and transported them away. There is no direct evidence on point, but the original e-mail from Arillotta supports Recovery's assertion. ("[I] suggest work at the existing location of the rail cars."). There is no evidence proffered as to the current disposition of the scrap railcars (i.e., where they are) or their proceeds.

After delivery, CSX sent invoices for the scrap railcars totaling $115,757.36 addressed to IDEC at its Boston office (shared with Recovery). Nancy E. Marto ("Marto"), officer and registered agent of Recovery and "partner" in IDEC, states that, upon receipt of the invoices, she attempted several times to contact Whitehead to inquire about them. She says that Whitehead never returned her calls. This was apparently because Arillotta had told him not to speak to her.[1] Not until a check from Arillotta to CSX purporting to pay the invoices bounced did Whitehead call Marto.

Because Recovery and IDEC refused to pay CSX, CSX brought this action alleging (1) breach of contract, (2) account stated, (3) unjust enrichment, and (4) quantum meruit.

Whitehead states that "[a]t all times during [his] dealing with Mr. Arillotta, [he] believed [Arillotta] was representing, and authorized to act on behalf of, Recovery Express and Interstate Demolition." Whitehead apparently based this belief on the E-mail's domain name–recoveryexpress.com[2]–and the representations of Arillotta to him both in the E-mail and in subsequent telephone conversations. All invoices were addressed to IDEC, though Whitehead states that Arillotta represented that he was "acting on behalf of Recovery Express". "At no time prior to CSX's delivery of the rail cars ... did anyone inform [Whitehead] that Mr. Arillotta was not authorized to represent or transact business on behalf of either Recovery Express or Interstate Demolition."

Recovery claims that Arillotta never worked for it. How Arillotta acquired a Recovery e-mail address is explained thus: Marto and Thomas R. Trafton ("Trafton"), Recovery's President and Treasurer, became involved in another venture along with Arillotta and Dominic Ignagni–IDEC. Because of Marto's and Trafton's "personal interest in IDEC", the "fledgling" company was allowed to share the offices and some resources of Recovery, including telephones and facsimile machines–and, apparently, e-mail services. Other than physical resources, there is no evidence that Recovery ever shared anything with IDEC–assets, funds, books of business, bank accounts, or insurance coverage.

B. Procedural Posture

CSX filed its Complaint in October of 2004 alleging breach of contract by Recovery and IDEC and related equitable claims. IDEC is now defunct, and has made no appearance in this litigation. Recovery has moved for summary judgment.

---

[1] Interestingly, the reason IDEC has ceased to exist is because of fraud by Arillotta. It is unclear if the fraud is related to this case.

[2] With regard to e-mail addresses, the domain name is anything after the "@" symbol. It is a more user-friendly way of identifying the Internet protocol (IP) address needed by the computer network to deliver correctly the e-mail message. *See* Christopher G. Clark, *The Truth in Domain Names Act of 2003 and a Preventative Measure to Combat Typosquatting,* 89 CORNELL L. REV. 1476, 1483 & n. 40 (2004).

II. DISCUSSION

A. Contract (Legal) Claims

At base, what this case is about is CSX's attempt, having been duped by a fraudulent agent of Recovery, to shift the consequences of its own gullibility to someone else. The primary legal vehicle by which it seeks to do this is the contract doctrine of "apparent authority". "Apparent authority is the power held by an agent or other actor to affect a principal's legal relations with third parties when a third party reasonably believes the actor has authority to act on behalf of the principal and that belief is traceable to the principal's manifestations." RESTATEMENT (THIRD) OF AGENCY at § 2.03. It "is not established by the putative agent's words or conduct, but by those of the principal." *Rubel v. Hayden, Harding & Buchanan, Inc.,* 444 N.E.2d 1306 (Ma. App., 1983).

In what looks to be an issue of first impression, the facts of this case set up the question whether an e-mail domain name, by itself, cloaks a purported agent with authority sufficient as matter of law to be called "apparent". Because apparent authority depends on that knowledge held by Whitehead and CSX of Arillotta's authority, which knowledge was derived from actions of Recovery, the only relevant conduct by Recovery is that it issued Arillotta an e-mail address with its domain name. Such associations as Recovery having the same offices, mailing address, phone number, or fax number are red herrings; these facts–if Whitehead even possessed them prior to entering the contract– emanated from Arillotta by way of his e-mail signature or telephone representations. There is no evidence of the manifestation of those facts by Recovery to Whitehead and CSX (i.e., by way of its website, as CSX asserted at oral argument) until after the contract was entered and collection efforts had begun.[4]

The only act taken by Recovery known to Whitehead and CSX prior to entering the contract and upon which Whitehead could rely, was its issuance to Arillotta of an e-mail address sporting Recovery's domain name (@recoveryexpress.com). The Court holds that Whitehead and CSX were unreasonable, as matter of law, in their reliance solely on an e-mail domain name. Such a manifestation by Recovery cannot be sufficient to sustain a claim

---

[4] The same can be said for the authority conveyed by Arillotta's title at IDEC. Whatever authority a title may convey to a third party, nothing in the record indicates that Whitehead and CSX even knew what Arillotta's title was. *See* The E-mail (stating that Arillotta was "from" Recovery and IDEC); Whitehead Decl. ¶ 2 ("Mr. Arillotta told me that he was acting *on behalf of* Recovery Express ...." (emphasis added)). "If the third party ... is unaware of the agent's position ..., the principal is not accountable for the third party's belief in the agent's authority.... The third party may ... lack a basis reasonably to believe that the agent is authorized to bind the organization. Such a basis would be lacking, for instance, if the third party is unaware of the agent's position within the organization." Restatement at § 3.03, cmt. c.

of apparent authority. Granting an e-mail domain name, by itself, does not cloak the recipient with carte blanche authority to act on behalf the grantee. Were this so, every subordinate employee with a company e-mail address–down to the night watchman–could bind a company to the same contracts as the president. This is not the law.

Though e-mail communication may be relatively new to staid legal institutions, the results in analogous low-tech situations confirm this conclusion. The Court could find no cases where, for example, giving someone a business card with the company name or logo, access to a company car, or company stationery, *by themselves,* created sufficient indicia of apparent authority. *See Muscletech Research & Dev., Inc. v. East Coast Ingredients, LLC,* No. 00-CV-0753A(F), 2004 WL 941815, at *32 (W.D.N.Y. Mar. 25, 2004) (holding that issuance of a company credit card, business cards with company logo, possession of company paraphernalia, and appearing in company advertisements was insufficient to create apparent authority); *Asplund v. Selected Investments in Financial Equities, Inc.,* 103 Cal.Rptr.2d 34, 48-49 (2000) (issuance of a business card and display of a plaque insufficient to create apparent authority); *Raclaw v. Fay. Conmy and Co.,* 668 N.E.2d 114, 117 (1996) (permitting the occupation of offices, the use of telephones and receptionist, the receipt of mail at company offices, and access to stationery insufficient to create apparent authority); *McFarland v. Entergy Mississippi, Inc.,* 919 So.2d 894, 902, 2005 WL 2458870, at *6 (Miss.2005) (holding that putting a purported agent in electric company vehicle, when plaintiff knew that volunteers were assisting crews, was insufficient to create apparent authority); *Alexander v. Tom Chandler, ABS Global, Inc.,* 179 S.W.3d 385, 389-390 (Mo. App. 2005) (holding that providing nitrogen tanks with company logo, billing for services with invoices bearing company logo, sending postcards claiming to be a company representative, distributing business cards indicating representative status, and giving out calendars with company logo to be insufficient to create apparent authority); *Cowburn v. Leventis,* 619 S.E.2d 437, 448 (S.C., 2005) (holding that supplying forms and business cards were the only actions of defendant and were not sufficient to create apparent authority); *cf. Thesenga Land Co. v. Cirrus Warehouse, Inc.,* No. C5-03-370, 2003 WL 22889499, at *1-2 (Minn.App. Dec. 9, 2003) (finding support for apparent authority when agent used business card designating him as vice president and when agent met with representatives of plaintiff and directed and negotiated contract terms); *Dorna USA, LLC v. Lighthouse Superscreens, Inc.,* No. 02 Civ. 8973(RLC), 2004 WL 2721239, at *2 (S.D.N.Y. Nov. 29, 2004) (holding that sharing website and e-mail addresses, using identical business cards, and "collectively behav[ing] 'as a single production and sales team' ", as well as other facts "too numerous to detail" supported the existence of apparent authority).

An e-mail domain name is sufficiently analogous to business cards, company vehicles, and letterhead for these cases to be persuasive. Those indicia of apparent authority all convey some degree of association between the purported principal and agent. By themselves, however, no reasonable person could conclude that apparent authority was present. The same is true with e-mail domain names.

In the end, CSX and Whitehead should have been more suspicious of an unsolicited, poorly written e-mail that arrived late one Friday afternoon. There are means by which CSX could have protected itself (e.g., requiring a purchase order form from IDEC or Recovery). Before delivering goods worth over $115,000 to a stranger, one reasonably should be expected to inquire as to the authority of that person to have made such a deal. Given the anonymity of the Internet, this case illustrates the potential consequences of operating–even in today's fast-paced business world–as did CSX.

III. CONCLUSION

Because there is no genuine issue of material fact as to whether Arillotta possessed the apparent authority of Recovery to enter into a contract with CSX– he did not possess such authority–and because there is no evidence that Recovery had the benefit of CSX's railcars, Recovery's Motion for Summary Judgment is ALLOWED and judgment will enter for it.

Notes and Questions

1. Reality Check

a. Why did the court hold that Mr. Arillotta did not have apparent authority?

b. Did Recovery do anything that might reasonably lead CSX to believe that Arillotta was authorized to enter into the railcar transaction?

2. Suppose

a. Suppose CSX had contacted Recovery, trying to reach Mr. Arillotta, and Recovery put the two in touch with one another. Would that create apparent authority in Mr. Arillotta?

3. What Do You Think?

a. Is the court correct in its holding? Why shouldn't providing an agent with business cards create at least some apparent authority? Shouldn't providing an email account be treated the same way?

4. You Draft It

a. The medium makes a difference. Redraft the email so that it would be appropriate for a business letter. Then redraft it so that it would be appropriate for a business email. Then redraft it so that it would be appropriate for a business IM. The text of the email follows:

From: Albert Arillotta [albert@recoveryexpress.com]
Sent: Friday, August 22, 2003 4:57 PM
To: Whitehead, Len Jr.
Subject: purchase of out service railcars

lynn this is albert arillotta from interstate demolition and recovery express we are interested in buying rail cars for scrap paying you a percentage of what the amm maket indicator is there are several locations i suggest to work at the exsisting location of the rail cars. we will send you a brochure and financials per your request our address is the following:
interstate demolition/recoveryexpress
180 canal street 5th floor boston mass 02114
phone number 617-523-7740
fax number 617-367-3627
email address albert @recoveryexpress.com

thank you for your time

Page 99

The last line of the second full paragraph should read:
rather than *unidentified principal*.

Chapter 5
The Incorporation Process

Page 124

Add the following sentence after the first sentence in the paragraph of
"1. Reserving the Name":

Effective August 1, 2006, Delaware added § 102(e), which permits a name to be
reserved for 120 days.

Chapter 7
Cashing Out: Distributing Money to Shareholders

Page 209
Line 2, change § 8.31 to § 8.33.

Page 211
Replace the second paragraph of *McIlvaine v. AmSouth Bank, N.A.* with:
   AmSouth also alleged that Tommy was survived by a ... son named Eugene Thomas McIlvaine III (Gene) .... The trial court instructed the trustee to pay the April 11, 1989, dividend to [Tommy's widow] Dorothy J. McIlvaine as executrix of Tommy's estate .... Gene appeals.

Page 218
Replace the second paragraph of *Reiss v. Financial Performance Corporation* with:
   [In 1993,] the Board of Directors of defendant Financial Performance Corporation (Financial), [issued] a warrant to Rebot Corporation, permitting Rebot to purchase 1,198,904 shares of Financial's common stock at a price of 10 cents per share. The warrant was executed in consideration of a $187,328.79 loan that Financial was unable to repay to Rebot. [F]inancial's Board also gave authorization to issue a warrant to Marvin Reiss (who was, at the time, a member of Financial's Board and apparently Rebot's President), permitting him to purchase 500,000 shares of stock at 10 cents per share. This warrant was issued as an honorarium payment for Reiss' services on Financial's Board. Both the Rebot and Reiss warrants provided that the right to purchase stock would extend for a period of five years ....

Page 225
Replace the second paragraph of *In the Matter of the Estate of Dudley B. Dawson* with:
   In three prior intermediate accountings, the Chancery Division, Probate Part, had defined the term "stock dividend" by referring to the traditional rule,

which focuses on a capitalization of assets. Accordingly, in those earlier accountings that court had allocated stock distributions to income whenever the issuing corporation [transferred] assets from a surplus account to a capital account. In the fourth intermediate accounting, however, the trial court adopted a different test to distinguish between stock dividends and stock splits. Adopting the New York Stock Exchange rule, the trial court characterized stock distributions as dividends if they constituted less than twenty-five percent of the outstanding shares of stock and as splits if they equaled twenty-five percent or more of the outstanding shares. In an unpublished opinion, the Appellate Division reversed the trial court's judgment, rejecting that court's twenty-five-percent rule and relying instead on the traditional approach. We granted certification to determine the correct rule.

On December 1, 1952, the testator, Dudley Dawson, executed a will. At that time, he was married to his second wife, Anna Coffin Dawson. Dudley Dawson died on May 11, 1957. Paragraph "TWENTIETH" established a ... trust, instructing the trustees to (1) pay the entire net annual income from the trust to Anna during her life ...; and (2) pay the income from the trust after Anna's death to "my nieces and nephews, and the issue of any deceased niece or nephew, * * * in equal shares per stirpes * * *." The will provided that the trust would exist as long as the rule against perpetuities ... would allow, namely, twenty-one years after the death of the survivor of the named niece, nephew, grandniece, and three grandnephews. The trustees were directed to distribute the trust funds thereafter "to my nieces and nephews and the issue of any deceased niece or nephew, in equal shares per stirpes * * *." Paragraphs "THIRTY-FOURTH" and "THIRTY-FIFTH" named Dawson's wife, Anna, and the Hanover Bank (later Manufacturers Hanover Trust Company, and currently Chemical Bank) as executors and trustees.

After the death of Anna Coffin Dawson in September 1989, the trustees filed with the Chancery Division a fourth intermediate accounting, running from May 12, 1981, to September 3, 1989 .... The court, now presided over by a different judge from the one who had heard the previous applications, appointed a new guardian *ad litem* to represent the interests of the minor defendants (the guardian *ad litem* who had represented their interests in the previous accountings had died), and extended the guardian *ad litem*'s representation to include the unborn parties in interest. That new guardian *ad litem* then challenged the trustees' proposed allocation to income of eight stock distributions that the trust had received during the period of the fourth intermediate accounting. All the disputed stock distributions involved transfers of funds to the issuing corporations' capital-stock accounts, but the guardian *ad litem* urged the court to adopt a new rule in respect of how to determine whether a stock distribution is a dividend or a split.

Chapter 8
Getting Money to Creditors When the Corporation Can't Pay

Page 296
Insert the following before "**3. Commercial and Bankruptcy Doctrines**":

When the claim against the subsidiary corporation sounds in tort, can the plaintiff hold the corporate parent liable on the ground that the parent's business plan for the subsidiary was a proximate cause of the harm to the plaintiff? The next case takes up this question.

Forsythe v. Clark USA, Inc.
864 N.E.2d 227 (Ill. 2007)

Justice GARMAN delivered the judgment of the court, with opinion:

On March 13, 1995, Michael F. Forsythe and Gary Szabla, mechanics at a refinery owned and operated by Clark Refining and Marketing (Clark Refining), were killed. The estate of each decedent received payment from Clark Refining pursuant to the Workers' Compensation Act. In 1996 and 1997, plaintiffs Marguerite Forsythe and Elizabeth Szabla, as special administrators of the estates of their late husbands, filed suits against Clark Refining and other defendants. Subsequently, plaintiffs added Clark Refining's parent company, Clark USA, as a defendant.

Clark USA is the only defendant involved in this appeal. At the close of discovery, the trial court granted Clark USA's motion for summary judgment …. The trial court did not state its reasoning. Plaintiffs appealed, and the appellate court reversed and remanded. Following that decision, defendant petitioned this court for leave to appeal ….

We granted defendant's petition to consider … whether a parent company can be held liable under a theory of direct participant liability for controlling its subsidiary's budget in a way that led to a workplace accident….

BACKGROUND

Clark Refining operated an oil refinery in Blue Island, Illinois. Defendant is Clark Refining's parent company and sole shareholder. On March 13, 1995, decedents were on their lunch break when a fire broke out at the refinery, killing them both. The fire was apparently caused when other Clark Refining employees attempted to replace a valve on a pipe without ensuring that flammable materials within the pipe had been depressurized. Plaintiffs claim that those employees were not maintenance mechanics and were not trained or qualified to perform the work they were attempting.

Plaintiffs' allegations of liability center around defendant's overall budgetary strategy. Specifically, plaintiffs allege that defendant breached a duty to use reasonable care in imposing its business strategy on Clark Refining by (1) "requiring [Clark Refining] to minimize operating costs including costs for training, maintenance, supervision and safety," (2) "requiring [Clark Refining] to limit capital investments to those which would generate cash for the refinery thereby preventing [Clark Refining] from adequately reinforcing the walls of the lunchroom or relocating the lunchroom to a safe position within the refinery," and (3) "failing to adequately evaluate the safety and training procedures in place at the Blue Island Refinery." Moreover, plaintiffs allege that defendant's strategy of capital cutbacks forced Clark Refining to have unqualified employees act as maintenance mechanics which, in turn, led to the fire that killed the decedents. This, plaintiffs argue, constitutes proximate cause.

In support of its motion for summary judgment, defendant contended that it owed no duty to either decedent by virtue of its status as a mere holding company, which was connected to Clark Refining only as a shareholder. Defendant submitted evidence to prove that Clark Refining owned and operated the refinery while defendant itself had no control over the day-to-day operations. Plaintiffs countered that defendant was directly responsible for creating conditions that precipitated the accident.

In support of their argument, plaintiffs cited evidence that defendant's directors created and approved Clark Refining's budget, striving to "position itself as a low cost refiner and marketer" with the goal of replenishing defendant's cash reserve by "decreas[ing] capital spending * * * to minimum sustainable levels" through the institution of a "survival mode" business plan. Plaintiffs also produced evidence that the boards of directors of Clark Refining and defendant met simultaneously. Moreover, plaintiffs relied upon evidence that the belt-tightening budget created by Clark Refining was overseen by Paul Melnuk, who served as defendant's president as well as chief executive officer of Clark Refining.

ANALYSIS

I. Direct Participant Liability

To state a cause of action for negligence, plaintiffs must show that defendant owed and breached a duty of care, proximately causing the plaintiffs injury. The threshold issue in this case is the existence of a duty, which is a question of law for the court to decide. [T]he touchstone of this court's duty analysis is to ask whether a plaintiff and a defendant stood in such a relationship to one another that the law imposed upon the defendant an obligation of reasonable conduct for the benefit of the plaintiff. Four factors inform this inquiry: (1) the reasonable foreseeability of injury, (2) the likelihood of injury, (3) the magnitude of the burden of guarding against the injury, and (4) the consequences of placing the burden upon the defendant.

Before undertaking our analysis, we note, as did the parties and the appellate court, that the theory of direct participant liability presented here has not previously been addressed in Illinois. It has been addressed in other states and throughout the federal courts, however. We will consider this authority where appropriate in our analysis.

Plaintiffs argue that defendant demanded Clark Refining operate its refinery pursuant to an overall business strategy that it knew would adversely affect safety by forcing reductions in training and maintenance. Indeed, plaintiffs contend that defendant actively and directly mandated unreasonable cuts in Clark Refining's budget in order to carry out its strategy. This strategy was outlined in Clark USA business records calling for a "survival mode" business philosophy accomplished through "reduced capital spending," "reduced working capital investment," and "reduced operating expense level." Plaintiffs allege that this "survival mode" strategy was mandated, despite the fact that defendant knew or should have known that the only feasible budget cuts would come from safety, maintenance, and training expenses. This, plaintiffs' conclude, constitutes direct participation by defendant in the harm caused. As such, plaintiffs contend the appellate court correctly found that defendant owed them a duty based on the direct participant theory and not on the legal relationship of defendant to its subsidiary.

Defendant contends that unless the standards for piercing the corporate veil are met, a parent company cannot be held liable for the negligence of its subsidiary. Attendant to that rule is the principle that a parent company does not owe a duty to third parties to supervise or control the conduct of its subsidiary to ensure that the subsidiary acts with reasonable care. Clark Refining owed a nondelegable duty to its employees to provide them with a safe workplace while defendant, as a parent, owed no duty whatsoever to ensure that Clark Refining met its obligations.

Additionally, even if direct liability is a recognized theory of recovery, defendant argues that the simple task of setting financial goals and employing an overall strategy to meet those goals is not improper but, instead, is "consistent with the parent's investor status" and thus "should not give rise to direct liability." *United States v. Bestfoods,* 524 U.S. 51, 69 (1998). Because its conduct was always consistent with its investor status, defendant claims, there is no basis to treat it as a direct participant in the negligence alleged herein.

While the Supreme Court has held that "[i]t is a general principle * * * deeply 'ingrained in our economic and legal systems' that a parent corporation * * * is not liable for the acts of its subsidiaries" (*Bestfoods,* 524 U.S. at 61, quoting W.O. Douglas & C. Shanks, *Insulation from Liability Through Subsidiary Corporations,* 39 YALE L.J. 193 (1929)), a significant body of case law supports the direct participant theory of liability urged by the plaintiffs. Some of that authority relies on the 1929 article quoted above and written, in relevant part, by then-Professor William O. Douglas.

Douglas noted that liability has been imposed in "instances where the parent is directly a participant in the wrong complained of." 39 YALE L.J. at 208. In such instances, "the use of the latent power incident to stock ownership to accomplish a specific result made the parent a participator in or doer of the act," specifically evident where "there was interference in the internal management of the subsidiary; an overriding of the discretion of the managers of the subsidiary." 39 YALE L.J. at 209. Douglas stated further that "direct intervention or intermeddling by the parent in the affairs of the subsidiary and more particularly in the transaction involved, to the disregard of the normal and orderly procedure of corporate control carried out through the election of the desired directors and officers of the subsidiary and the handling by them of the direction of its affairs, seems to have been determinative in some cases to holding the parent liable." 39 YALE L.J. at 218.

The United States Supreme Court quoted the Douglas & Shanks article approvingly in *Bestfoods,* 524 U.S. at 64-65. The Court noted that the simple fact that directors of a parent corporation serve as directors of its subsidiary does not, standing alone, expose the parent corporation to liability for its subsidiary's acts. *Bestfoods,* 524 U.S. at 69-70. The Court went on to state, however, that "the acts of direct operation that give rise to parental liability must necessarily be distinguished from the interference that stems from the normal relationship between parent and subsidiary," and "[t]he critical question is whether, in degree and detail, actions directed to the facility by an agent of the parent alone are eccentric under accepted norms of parental oversight of a subsidiary's facility." *Bestfoods,* 524 U.S. at 71-72.

Similarly, in *Esmark, Inc. v. National Labor Relations Board,* 887 F.2d 739 (7th Cir.1989), the Seventh Circuit, in a case dealing with a potential violation of the National Labor Relations Act, cited Douglas & Shanks' article extensively and noted that Judge Learned Hand also recognized that a parent corporation could be held liable for the actions of its subsidiaries if the parent directly supervised the conduct of a specific transaction. In *Kingston Dry Dock Co. v. Lake Champlain Transportation Co.,* 31 F.2d 265, 267 (2d Cir.1929),

Judge Hand wrote that such liability "normally must depend upon the parent's direct intervention in the transaction, ignoring the subsidiary's paraphernalia of incorporation, directors and officers." Relying on that authority, the Seventh Circuit held that "a parent corporation may be held liable for the wrongdoing of a subsidiary where the parent directly participated in the subsidiary's unlawful actions." *Esmark,* 887 F.2d at 756.

Moreover, the court held that "[w]here the parent specifically directs the actions of its subsidiary, using its ownership interest to command rather than merely cajole," the possibility of direct liability is present and will be imposed "where a parent disregards the separate legal personality of its subsidiary (and the subsidiary's own decisionmaking 'paraphernalia'), and exercises direct control over a specific transaction." *Esmark,* 887 F.2d at 757. The court described this as a "transaction-specific" theory of direct participation, citing numerous cases where parent companies have been held liable for misconduct by their subsidiaries. *Esmark,* 887 F.2d at 756 (collecting cases). Under this "transaction-specific" theory, shareholders or parent corporations are not held directly liable for their own independently wrongful acts but, instead, for their actions against third-party interests through the agency of subsidiaries. *Esmark,* 887 F.2d at 756. Accordingly, the court held that a parent corporation can be liable for interposing a guiding hand in the transactions of its subsidiary. *Esmark,* 887 F.2d at 756.

Plaintiffs also cite other cases approving of direct liability. In *Papa v. Katy Industries, Inc.,* 166 F.3d 937, 941 (7th Cir.1999), the Seventh Circuit, again interpreting the National Labor Relations Act, evinced its continuing support for direct participant liability when it cited *Esmark, Bestfoods,* and *Kingston Dry Dock* to state "that limited liability does not protect a parent corporation when the parent is sought to be held liable for its own act, rather than merely as the owner of the subsidiary that acted." Similarly, in *Pearson v. Component Technology Corp.,* [247 F.3d 471 (3d Cir.2001)], the Third Circuit, interpreting federal law, stated that "[a]lthough not often employed * * * it has long been acknowledged that parents may be 'directly' liable for their subsidiaries' actions when the 'alleged wrong can seemingly be traced to the parent through the conduit of its own personnel and management,' and the parent has interfered with the subsidiary's operations in a way that surpasses the control exercised by a parent as an incident of ownership." *Pearson,* 247 F.3d at 486-87 (3d Cir.2001), citing *Bestfoods,* 524 U.S. at 64, quoting 39 YALE L.J. at 207. Likewise, in *Boggs v. Blue Diamond Coal Co.,* 590 F.2d 655, 663 (6th Cir.1979), the Sixth Circuit, interpreting Kentucky law, implicitly indicated its recognition of direct liability when it stated that "a parent is not immune from tort liability to its subsidiary employees for its own, independent acts of negligence."

The Indiana Supreme Court, in *Commissioner of Department of Environmental Management v. RLG, Inc.,* 755 N.E.2d 556, 559, 563 (Ind. 2001), also accepted direct participant liability when it held a defendant's sole officer and shareholder liable for violations of Indiana environmental laws and stated that "an individual, though acting in a corporate capacity * * * may be individually liable * * * as a direct participant under general legal principles." Additionally, the Iowa Supreme Court accepted a direct participant theory of liability when it held that a member of a limited liability corporation could be sued because it had undertaken to perform management services for the corporation and allegedly performed those services negligently. *Estate of Countryman v. Farmers Cooperative Ass'n,* 679 N.W.2d 598, 605 (Iowa 2004). Other courts have also accepted the theory of direct participant liability. See, *e.g., United States v. TIC Investment Corp.,* 68 F.3d 1082, 1091 n. 9 (8th Cir.1995) (interpreting the Comprehensive Environmental Response, Compensation, and Liability Act, the court held that "a parent corporation may be directly liable for activities carried out ostensibly by its subsidiary if the parent corporation, in effect, actually operated the subsidiary's facility by having the authority to control and actually or substantially controlling the facility"); *United States v. Kayser-Roth Corp.,* 910 F.2d 24, 27 (1st Cir.1990) (parent corporation can be held directly liable if actively involved in the affairs of its subsidiary); *Dassault Falcon Jet Corp. v. Oberflex, Inc.,* 909 F.Supp. 345, 347, 354 (M.D.N.C.1995) (direct participant liability could be maintained against a parent company for breach of warranty). Taken together, these cases make evident the substantial weight of authority supporting recognition of this theory of liability.

In opposition to plaintiffs' theory, defendant contends that a parent corporation owes no duty to supervise its subsidiary's conduct for the benefit of third parties. Defendant cites *Young v. Bryco Arms,* 821 N.E.2d 1078 (Ill. 2004), where this court noted its recognition of the general rule that "one has no duty to control the conduct of another to prevent him from causing harm to a third party, absent a special relationship with either the person causing the harm or the injured party." Building on that point, defendant argues that courts have uniformly rejected the argument that the parent-subsidiary relationship qualifies as the kind of "special relationship" necessary to give rise to a duty to supervise or control the conduct of the subsidiary. *In re Birmingham Asbestos Litigation,* 619 So.2d 1360 (Ala.1993). Supporting this contention, defendant cites *Joiner v. Ryder System Inc.,* 966 F.Supp. 1478 (C.D.Ill.1996), where the district court applied Illinois law and concluded that a duty could not be predicated either on the parent's ability to control its subsidiary or on its actual exercise of control:

> "RSI–as every parent corporation does–obviously has the power to control its subsidiaries. In fact, RSI owns them and RSI can 'force' them to do anything it wants. That power, by itself, however, does not impose a duty upon RSI. Only if RSI abused the power–by exerting too much control–could it be held liable for the conduct of its subsidiaries as an alter ego." *Joiner,* 966 F.Supp. at 1490.

Additionally, defendant contends that direct participant claims virtually identical to those raised here were rejected by two state appellate decisions, one from Texas and one from California. In *Coastal Corp. v. Torres,* 133 S.W.3d 776 (Tex.App.2004), refinery employees injured in an explosion brought a negligence action against the refinery's parent company. The employees alleged that " 'through central budgetary authority exercised by Coastal's corporate officers * * * Coastal * * * assumed control over maintenance, turnaround, and inspection matters at the plant,' " limited expenditures, and "controlled and influenced its subsidiary in a way that directly resulted in appellees' injuries." *Coastal Corp.,* 133 S.W.3d at 777, 779. The *Coastal Corp.* court noted that the plaintiffs in that case alleged "negligent control of the budget, not negligent control over details of specific operational activities," and eventually found that the parent company had no duty as a matter of Texas law to "approve budgets for its subsidiaries in order to assure that the subsidiaries repair defects on their premises." *Coastal Corp.,* 133 S.W.3d at 779, 782.

Similarly, in *Waste Management Inc. v. Superior Court of San Diego,* 13 Cal.Rptr.3d 910, (Cal.App. 2004), plaintiffs brought an action against a parent company for negligently controlling its subsidiary's budget such that the subsidiary was prevented from replacing and repairing trash trucks. The court recognized direct participant liability and stated that "the parent may owe a duty arising out of obligations independent of the parent subsidiary relationship." *Waste Management,* 13 Cal.Rptr.3d 910. The court went on to hold, however, that "[n]egligently controlling or intentionally mismanaging a subsidiary's budget does not create a duty on the part of the parent corporation to ensure safety or prevent injuries to the subsidiary's employees." *Waste Management,* 13 Cal.Rptr.3d 910.

As defendant points out, *Coastal Corp.* and *Waste Management* stand for the proposition that mere budgetary mismanagement is not enough to support direct participant liability. Additionally, however, the *Coastal Corp.* court noted that "it is apparent that liability is imposed when there is specific control over the activity that caused the accident." *Coastal Corp.,* 133 S.W.3d at 779. Similarly, the *Waste Management* court stated that the plaintiffs' case failed because they could not show that the parent company "directed and authorized the *manner* in which the subsidiary conducted its business." (Emphasis in original). *Waste Management,* 13 Cal.Rptr.3d 910. In other words, these courts found that a viable claim of liability under the direct participant theory cannot rest solely upon budgetary mismanagement, but budgetary mismanagement can make up one part of a viable claim, in conjunction with the direction or authorization of the manner in which an activity is undertaken. The *Joiner* decision echoes this sentiment. There, the court granted summary judgment in favor of the parent/defendant, noting significantly that the parent/defendant did "not get involved in the day-to-day activities or management of the subsidiaries." *Joiner,* 966 F.Supp. at 1490. Based upon this analysis, we conclude that budgetary mismanagement, accompanied by the parent's negligent direction or authorization of the manner in which the subsidiary accomplishes that budget, can lead to a valid cause of action under the direct participant theory of liability.

Considering the above, we hold that direct participant liability is a valid theory of recovery under Illinois law. Where there is evidence sufficient to prove that a parent company mandated an overall business and budgetary strategy *and* carried that strategy out by its own specific direction or authorization, surpassing the control exercised as a normal incident of ownership in disregard for the interests of the subsidiary, that parent company could face liability. The key elements to the application of direct participant liability, then, are a parent's specific direction or authorization of the manner in which an activity is undertaken and foreseeability. If a parent company specifically directs an activity, where injury is foreseeable, that parent could be held liable. Similarly, if a parent company mandates an overall course of action and then authorizes the manner in which specific activities contributing to that course of action are undertaken, it can be liable for foreseeable injuries. We again stress, though, that allegations of mere budgetary mismanagement alone do not give rise to the application of direct participant liability.

Our finding is supported by the policy-based factors courts use to determine whether a duty exists. *Marshall v. Burger King Corp.*, 856 N.E.2d 1048 (Ill. 2006) (the factors are (1) the reasonable foreseeability of injury, (2) the likelihood of injury, (3) the magnitude of the burden of guarding against the injury, and (4) the consequences of placing the burden upon the defendant). Certain heavy industries, like refining, inherently involve a great amount of danger. It is conceivable that severe cutbacks in staffing, safety, maintenance, and training in such industries could lead, with reasonable foreseeability, to the injury of others. The likelihood of injury in those circumstances would not be remote and could be deadly. Additionally, the magnitude of the burden of guarding against such injury would not be great. Parent companies are free to craft overall business and budgetary strategies; such companies simply must not interfere directly in the manner their subsidiaries undertake certain activities such that the subsidiaries are no longer free to utilize their own expertise. Alternatively, if parent companies do interfere directly in the manner their subsidiaries undertake certain activities, they must do so with reasonable care. Finally, it is not an undue burden to require that parent corporations engage in the considered exercise of due care in an already limited role. As we have already acknowledged, parent corporations are generally not liable for the acts of their subsidiaries. *Bestfoods*, 524 U.S. at 61, quoting 39 YALE L.J. 193 (1929). Moreover, the mere fact of a parent-subsidiary relationship, without a great deal more, does not give rise to liability. *Bestfoods*, 524 U.S. at 61, quoting 1 W. FLETCHER, CYCLOPEDIA OF LAW OF PRIVATE CORPORATIONS § 33, at 568 (rev.ed.1990).

This court has repeatedly and consistently highlighted the point that it is "axiomatic that every person owes to all others a duty to exercise ordinary care to guard against injury which naturally flows as a reasonably probable and foreseeable consequence of his act." *Frye v. Medicare-Glaser Corp.*, 605 N.E.2d 557 (Ill. 1992), quoting *Nelson v. Union Wire Rope Corp.*, 199 N.E.2d 769 (Ill. 1964); see also *Mt. Zion State Bank & Trust v. Consolidated Communications, Inc.*, 660 N.E.2d 863 (Ill. 1995); *Widlowski v. Durkee*, 562 N.E.2d 967 (Ill. 1990); *Feldscher v. E & B, Inc.*, 447 N.E.2d 1331 (Ill. 1983). Recognizing that a parent company may have a duty based upon direct participant liability does not end the analysis though. Certain facts must still be present to give rise to its application.

II. Direct Participant Liability Applied

Returning to the specific issue in this case, we must resolve whether there exists a question of material fact such that the evidence presented could lead a reasonable observer to believe that defendant's overall business and budgetary strategy involved the negligent direction or authorization of the manner in which Clark Refining conducted its business. If so, the trial court's grant of summary judgment was inappropriate.

Defendant's overall business strategy at the time of the tragic accident involved here mandated increased productivity driven, at least in part, by budgetary cuts. The question remains, though, whether those cuts were negligently directed by or conducted in a manner authorized by defendant at the expense of Clark Refining. Answering this question requires a close look at the role of defendant's president, Paul Melnuk, who also served as chief executive officer of Clark Refining.

In *Bestfoods*, the Supreme Court pointed out that lower courts must "recognize that 'it is entirely appropriate for directors of a parent corporation to serve as directors of its subsidiary, and that fact alone may not serve to expose the parent corporation to liability for its subsidiary's acts.' " *Bestfoods*, 524 U.S. at 69, citing *American Protein Corp. v. AB Volvo*, 844 F.2d 56, 57 (2d Cir.1988). The Court acknowledged the " 'well established principle [of corporate law] that directors and officers holding positions with a parent and its subsidiary can and do "change hats" to represent the two corporations separately, despite their common ownership.' " *Bestfoods*, 524 U.S. at 69, citing *Lusk v. Foxmeyer Health Corp.*, 129 F.3d 773, 779 (5th Cir.1997). Further, the Court noted that it should be presumed that directors are wearing their "subsidiary hats," rather than their "parent hats," when acting for the subsidiary. *Bestfoods*, 524 U.S. at 69.

Accordingly, to establish liability, plaintiffs must establish more than the fact that Paul Melnuk made policy decisions and supervised subsidiary activities. *Bestfoods*, 524 U.S. at 69. Instead, plaintiffs must show that the conduct complained of occurred while Paul Melnuk was acting in his capacity as an officer of Clark USA, rather than as an officer of Clark Refining. *Bestfoods*,

524 U.S. at 69. In attempting to do so, plaintiffs point to additional language from *Bestfoods,* where the Court stated that "the presumption that an act is taken on behalf of the corporation for whom the officer claims to act is strongest when the act is perfectly consistent with the norms of corporate behavior, but wanes as the distance from those accepted norms approaches the point of action by a dual officer plainly contrary to the interests of the subsidiary yet nonetheless advantageous to the parent." *Bestfoods,* 524 U.S. at 70 n. 13.

Seizing upon that language, plaintiffs point to the April 1995 "Memorandum to the Executive Committee," prepared by Paul Melnuk, completed on Clark USA letterhead, and including a document entitled "1995 Economic Imperatives." Moreover, plaintiffs point to another Clark USA business record, the agenda for the February 15, 1995, board of directors meeting, which includes a section entitled "Clark USA Liquidity Overview." That document lays out a "survival mode" business philosophy marked by "reduced capital spending," "reduced working capital investment," and "reduced operating expense level." The document further states that the "goal is to replenish [defendant's] strategic cash reserve to $200 million." Defendant's continued emphasis on this goal is supported by the "1995 Economic Imperatives," one of which was to "[r]eplenish cash balance to 200 million" by reducing capital spending to "minimum sustainable levels." Relying on this, plaintiffs contend that the business and budgetary strategy defendant mandated in this case was carried out for its own benefit at the foreseeable expense of safety and spending at Clark Refining and at the direction of Paul Melnuk. As such, the only benefit of the business and budgetary strategy involved in this case ran to defendant and not Clark Refining. This, plaintiffs argue, proves that Paul Melnuk was acting not on behalf of Clark Refining but, instead, on behalf of Clark USA.

In opposition, defendant cites the testimony of Paul Melnuk himself where he claims that the 1995 Imperatives, though completed on defendant's letterhead, were actually carried out for Clark Refining. Additionally, defendant notes that the 1995 Imperatives include discussion of the continuing need to spend on necessary health and safety as well as ensure that all existing environmental, health, and safety needs are fully supported.

At the very least, there is a genuine issue of material fact as to whose "hat" Melnuk was wearing when he completed the 1995 memorandum. If the fact finder concludes that Melnuk was acting on behalf of defendant and thus wearing his Clark USA "hat," there is some evidence that he was directing or authorizing the manner in which Clark Refining's budget was implemented such that he had a duty, under the direct participant theory of liability, to do so with reasonable care. The additional evidence produced by plaintiffs indicating that Melnuk knew both that the budgetary reductions involved here had to come in large part from controllable costs such as education, training, repairs, and equipment maintenance, and that these reductions were compromising safety at the refinery raises an issue of material fact as to whether or not defendant breached that duty. The trial court's grant of summary judgment was therefore inappropriate.

If Paul Melnuk, acting on behalf of defendant, directed or authorized the manner in which the budget cuts in this case were taken, he had a duty to do so in a nonnegligent way. If Melnuk directed or authorized the manner in which the budget cuts at issues were taken, knowing that safety at the Blue Island refinery would be compromised, and did so superseding the discretion and interest of Clark Refining, direct participant liability could attach. Determining whether this duty applies to the facts of this case, and whether defendant is liable, involves factual inquiry. This inquiry is not suitable for this court on review and not appropriate for disposition at summary judgment, especially considering that this court must interpret the record strictly against the moving party and liberally in favor of the nonmoving party.

CONCLUSION

Drawing no ultimate conclusions on the merits of plaintiffs' case and mindful that summary judgment is an extraordinary remedy, summary judgment was inappropriate in this matter. We recognize the direct participant theory of liability. We note, however, that this theory of liability gives rise to a duty only in limited circumstances. Budgetary oversight alone is insufficient, as is a parent company's commission of acts consistent with its investor status.

If there is sufficient evidence to show that a parent corporation directed or authorized the manner in which an activity is undertaken, however, a duty arises. Specifically, the duty to utilize reasonable care in directing or authorizing the manner in which that activity is undertaken. Accordingly, a parent corporation can be held liable if, for its own benefit, it directs or authorizes the manner in which its subsidiary's budget is implemented, disregarding the discretion and interests of the subsidiary, and thereby creating dangerous conditions.

For these reasons, we affirm the appellate court's reversal of the trial court's grant of summary judgment and its remand of the cause to the circuit court for further proceedings.

Notes and Questions

1. Reality Check

a. What was the plaintiffs' theory of liability? What are its elements?

b. Why did the court accept the plaintiffs' theory? What reservations did the court have?

2. Suppose

a. Suppose it were clear that Mr. Melnuk was acting solely for Clark Refining. Would that make the plaintiffs' case stronger or weaker?

b. Suppose it were clear that Mr. Melnuk was acting solely for Clark USA. Would that make the plaintiffs' case stronger or weaker?

3. What Do You Think?

a. Do you believe that Clark USA was a direct participant in causing the deaths of the workers?

b. Should an owner's business and financial plan for its business render the owner liable for the business's physical torts?

Page 305

Add the following Note:

a. The briefs state that the ladder was fabricated and installed in 1983 and that Mr. Pancratz was injured in June 1991.

Chapter 10
Restrictions on the Board's Power

Page 359
Delete the last sentence of the carryover paragraph.

Chapter 11
The Duty of Loyalty of Directors
(and Officers)

Page 383

Add the following sentence to the end of the third full paragraph:

Harris estimated the value of all the real estate at the time of the trial to be $1,550,000.

Page 394

Add the following before "**3. Trying to Generalize**":
(which will be renumbered in the second edition)

3. Failure to Monitor

Can directors violate their duty of loyalty when they do not "act" at all? That is, are there instances when the board's failure to consider any action may be seen as violating the requirement that "Each member of the board ... shall act ... in a manner the director reasonably believes to be in the best interest of the corporation"? The next case explores this possibility.

Stone v. Ritter
911 A.2d 362 (Del. 2006)

Before STEELE, Chief Justice, HOLLAND, BERGER, JACOBS, and RIDGELY, Justices (constituting the court *en banc*).

HOLLAND, J.:

This is an appeal from a final judgment of the Court of Chancery dismissing a derivative complaint against fifteen present and former directors of AmSouth Bancorporation ("AmSouth"), a Delaware corporation. The plaintiffs-appellants, William and Sandra Stone, are AmSouth shareholders and filed their derivative complaint without making a pre-suit demand on AmSouth's board of directors (the "Board"). The Court of Chancery held that the plaintiffs had failed to adequately plead that such a demand would have been futile. The Court, therefore, dismissed the derivative complaint under Court of Chancery Rule 23.1.

Facts

In 2004, AmSouth and AmSouth Bank paid $40 million in fines and $10 million in civil penalties to resolve government and regulatory investigations pertaining principally to the failure by bank employees to file "Suspicious Activity Reports" ("SARs"), as required by the federal Bank Secrecy Act ("BSA")[4] and various anti-money-laundering ("AML") regulations. Those investigations were conducted by the United States Attorney's Office for the Southern District of Mississippi ("USAO"), the Federal Reserve, FinCEN and the Alabama Banking Department. No fines or penalties were imposed on AmSouth's directors, and no other regulatory action was taken against them.

The government investigations arose originally from an unlawful "Ponzi" scheme operated by Louis D. Hamric, II and Victor G. Nance. In August 2000, Hamric, then a licensed attorney, and Nance, then a registered investment advisor with Mutual of New York, contacted an AmSouth branch bank in Tennessee to arrange for custodial trust accounts to be created for "investors" in a "business venture." That venture (Hamric and Nance represented) involved the construction of medical clinics overseas. In reality, Nance had convinced more than forty of his clients to invest in promissory notes bearing high rates of return, by misrepresenting the nature and the risk of that investment. Relying on similar misrepresentations by Hamric and Nance, the AmSouth branch employees in Tennessee agreed to provide custodial accounts for the investors and to distribute monthly interest payments to each account upon receipt of a check from Hamric and instructions from Nance.

The Hamric-Nance scheme was discovered in March 2002, when the investors did not receive their monthly interest payments. Thereafter, Hamric and Nance became the subject of several civil actions brought by the defrauded investors in Tennessee and Mississippi (and in which AmSouth also was named as a defendant), and also the subject of a federal grand jury investigation in the Southern District of Mississippi. Hamric and Nance were indicted on federal money-laundering charges, and both pled guilty.

---

[4] 31 U.S.C. § 5318 (2006) *et seq.* The Bank Secrecy Act and the regulations promulgated thereunder require banks to file with the Financial Crimes Enforcement Network, a bureau of the U.S. Department of the Treasury known as "FinCEN," a written "Suspicious Activity Report" (known as a "SAR") whenever, *inter alia,* a banking transaction involves at least $5,000 "and the bank knows, suspects, or has reason to suspect" that, among other possibilities, the "transaction involves funds derived from illegal activities or is intended or conducted in order to hide or disguise funds or assets derived from illegal activities." 31 U.S.C. § 5318(g) (2006); 31 C.F.R. § 103.18(a)(2) (2006).

On October 12, 2004, AmSouth and the USAO entered into a Deferred Prosecution Agreement ("DPA") in which AmSouth agreed: first, to the filing by USAO of a one-count Information in the United States District Court for the Southern District of Mississippi, charging AmSouth with failing to file SARs; and second, to pay a $40 million fine. In conjunction with the DPA, the USAO issued a "Statement of Facts," which noted that although in 2000 "at least one" AmSouth employee suspected that Hamric was involved in a possibly illegal scheme, AmSouth failed to file SARs in a timely manner. In neither the Statement of Facts nor anywhere else did the USAO ascribe any blame to the Board or to any individual director.

On October 12, 2004, the Federal Reserve and the Alabama Banking Department concurrently issued a Cease and Desist Order against AmSouth, requiring it, for the first time, to improve its BSA/AML program. That Cease and Desist Order required AmSouth to (among other things) engage an independent consultant "to conduct a comprehensive review of the Bank's AML Compliance program and make recommendations, as appropriate, for new policies and procedures to be implemented by the Bank." KPMG Forensic Services ("KPMG") performed the role of independent consultant and issued its report on December 10, 2004 (the "KPMG Report").

Also on October 12, 2004, FinCEN and the Federal Reserve jointly assessed a $10 million civil penalty against AmSouth for operating an inadequate anti-money-laundering program and for failing to file SARs. In connection with that assessment, FinCEN issued a written Assessment of Civil Money Penalty (the "Assessment"), which included detailed "determinations" regarding AmSouth's BSA compliance procedures. FinCEN found that "AmSouth violated the suspicious activity reporting requirements of the Bank Secrecy Act," and that "[s]ince April 24, 2002, AmSouth has been in violation of the anti-money-laundering program requirements of the Bank Secrecy Act." Among FinCEN's specific determinations were its conclusions that "AmSouth's [AML compliance] program lacked adequate board and management oversight," and that "reporting to management for the purposes of monitoring and oversight of compliance activities was materially deficient." AmSouth neither admitted nor denied FinCEN's determinations in this or any other forum.

Demand Futility and Director Independence

It is a fundamental principle of the Delaware General Corporation Law that "[t]he business and affairs of every corporation organized under this chapter shall be managed by or under the direction of a board of directors."[6] Thus, by its very nature [a] derivative action impinges on the managerial freedom of

---

[6] [DGCL] § 141(a).

directors. Therefore, the right of a stockholder to prosecute a derivative suit is limited to situations where either the stockholder has demanded the directors pursue a corporate claim and the directors have wrongfully refused to do so, or where demand is excused because the directors are incapable of making an impartial decision regarding whether to institute such litigation. Court of Chancery Rule 23.1, accordingly, requires that the complaint in a derivative action "allege with particularity the efforts, if any, made by the plaintiff to obtain the action the plaintiff desires from the directors [or] the reasons for the plaintiff's failure to obtain the action or for not making the effort."[9]

To excuse demand ... a court must determine whether or not the particularized factual allegations of a derivative stockholder complaint create a reasonable doubt that, as of the time the complaint is filed, the board of directors could have properly exercised its independent and disinterested business judgment in responding to a demand. The plaintiffs attempt to satisfy the ... test in this proceeding by asserting that the incumbent defendant directors face a substantial likelihood of liability that renders them personally interested in the outcome of the decision on whether to pursue the claims asserted in the complaint, and are therefore not disinterested or independent.

The standard for assessing a director's potential personal liability for failing to act in good faith in discharging his or her oversight responsibilities has evolved beginning with our decision in *Graham v. Allis-Chalmers Manufacturing Company,*[15] through the Court of Chancery's *Caremark* *decision to our most recent decision in *Disney.*[16] A brief discussion of that evolution will help illuminate the standard that we adopt in this case.

Graham *and* Caremark

Graham was a derivative action brought against the directors of Allis-Chalmers for failure to prevent violations of federal anti-trust laws by Allis-Chalmers employees. There was no claim that the Allis-Chalmers directors knew of the employees' conduct that resulted in the corporation's liability. Rather, the plaintiffs claimed that the Allis-Chalmers directors *should have known* of the illegal conduct by the corporation's employees. In *Graham,* this Court held that "*absent cause for suspicion* there is no duty upon the directors to install and

---

[9] Ch. Ct. R. 23.1. Allegations of demand futility under Rule 23.1 must comply with stringent requirements of factual particularity that differ substantially from the permissive notice pleadings governed solely by Chancery Rule 8(a).

[15] *Graham v. Allis-Chalmers Mfg. Co.,* 188 A.2d 125 (Del.1963).

* [*In re Caremark Int'l Litig.,* 698 A.2d 959 (Del. Ch. 1996).]

[16] *In re Walt Disney Co. Deriv. Litig.,* 906 A.2d 27 (Del.2006).

operate a corporate system of espionage to ferret out wrongdoing which they have no reason to suspect exists."[17]

In *Caremark*, the Court of Chancery reassessed the applicability of our holding in *Graham* when called upon to approve a settlement of a derivative lawsuit brought against the directors of Caremark International, Inc. The plaintiffs claimed that the Caremark directors should have known that certain officers and employees of Caremark were involved in violations of the federal Anti-Referral Payments Law. That law prohibits health care providers from paying any form of remuneration to induce the referral of Medicare or Medicaid patients. The plaintiffs claimed that the *Caremark* directors breached their fiduciary duty for having "allowed a situation to develop and continue which exposed the corporation to enormous legal liability and that in so doing they violated a duty to be active monitors of corporate performance."[18]

In evaluating whether to approve the proposed settlement agreement in *Caremark,* the Court of Chancery narrowly construed our holding in *Graham* "as standing for the proposition that, absent grounds to suspect deception, neither corporate boards nor senior officers can be charged with wrongdoing simply for assuming the integrity of employees and the honesty of their dealings on the company's behalf."[19] The *Caremark* Court opined it would be a "mistake" to interpret this Court's decision in *Graham* to mean that:

> corporate boards may satisfy their obligation to be reasonably informed concerning the corporation, without assuring themselves that information and reporting systems exist in the organization that are reasonably designed to provide to senior management and to the board itself timely, accurate information sufficient to allow management and the board, each within its scope, to reach informed judgments concerning both the corporation's compliance with law and its business performance.[20]

To the contrary, the *Caremark* Court stated, "it is important that the board exercise a good faith judgment that the corporation's information and reporting system is in concept and design adequate to assure the board that appropriate information will come to its attention in a timely manner as a matter of ordinary operations, so that it may satisfy its responsibility."[21] The *Caremark* Court recognized, however, that "the duty to act in good faith to be informed

---

[17] *Graham v. Allis-Chalmers Mfg. Co.,* 188 A.2d at 130 (emphasis added).

[18] *In re Caremark Int'l Inc. Deriv. Litig.,* 698 A.2d 959, 967 (Del.Ch.1996).

[19] *Id.* at 969.

[20] *Id.* at 970.

[21] *Id.*

cannot be thought to require directors to possess detailed information about all aspects of the operation of the enterprise."[22] The Court of Chancery then formulated the following standard for assessing the liability of directors where the directors are unaware of employee misconduct that results in the corporation being held liable:

> Generally where a claim of directorial liability for corporate loss is predicated upon ignorance of liability creating activities within the corporation, as in *Graham* or in this case, ... only a sustained or systematic failure of the board to exercise oversight–such as an utter failure to attempt to assure a reasonable information and reporting system exists–will establish the lack of good faith that is a necessary condition to liability.[23]

Caremark *Standard Approved*

As evidenced by the language quoted above, the *Caremark* standard for so-called "oversight" liability draws heavily upon the concept of director failure to act in good faith. That is consistent with the definition(s) of bad faith recently approved by this Court in its recent *Disney* decision, where we held that a failure to act in good faith requires conduct that is qualitatively different from, and more culpable than, the conduct giving rise to a violation of the fiduciary duty of care (i.e., gross negligence). In *Disney,* we identified the following examples of conduct that would establish a failure to act in good faith:

> A failure to act in good faith may be shown, for instance, where the fiduciary intentionally acts with a purpose other than that of advancing the best interests of the corporation, where the fiduciary acts with the intent to violate applicable positive law, or where the fiduciary intentionally fails to act in the face of a known duty to act, demonstrating a conscious disregard for his duties. There may be other examples of bad faith yet to be proven or alleged, but these three are the most salient.

The third of these examples describes, and is fully consistent with, the lack of good faith conduct that the *Caremark* court held was a "necessary condition" for director oversight liability, i.e., "a sustained or systematic failure of the board to exercise oversight–such as an utter failure to attempt to assure a reasonable information and reporting system exists...."[27] Indeed, our opinion in

---

[22] *Id.* at 971.

[23] *In re Caremark Int'l Inc. Deriv. Litig.*, 698 A.2d at 971.

[27] *In re Caremark Int'l Inc. Deriv. Litig.*, 698 A.2d 959, 971 (Del.Ch.1996).

Disney cited *Caremark* with approval for that proposition. Accordingly, the Court of Chancery applied the correct standard in assessing whether demand was excused in this case where failure to exercise oversight was the basis or theory of the plaintiffs' claim for relief.

It is important, in this context, to clarify a doctrinal issue that is critical to understanding fiduciary liability under *Caremark* as we construe that case. The phraseology used in *Caremark* and that we employ here–describing the lack of good faith as a "necessary condition to liability"–is deliberate. The purpose of that formulation is to communicate that a failure to act in good faith is not conduct that results, *ipso facto,* in the direct imposition of fiduciary liability.[29] The failure to act in good faith may result in liability because the requirement to act in good faith "is a subsidiary element[,]" i.e., a condition, "of the fundamental duty of loyalty."[30] It follows that because a showing of bad faith conduct, in the sense described in *Disney* and *Caremark,* is essential to establish director oversight liability, the fiduciary duty violated by that conduct is the duty of loyalty.

This view of a failure to act in good faith results in two additional doctrinal consequences. First, although good faith may be described colloquially as part of a "triad" of fiduciary duties that includes the duties of care and loyalty,[31] the obligation to act in good faith does not establish an independent fiduciary duty that stands on the same footing as the duties of care and loyalty. Only the latter two duties, where violated, may directly result in liability, whereas a failure to act in good faith may do so, but indirectly. The second doctrinal consequence is that the fiduciary duty of loyalty is not limited to cases involving a financial or other cognizable fiduciary conflict of interest. It also encompasses cases where the fiduciary fails to act in good faith. As the Court of Chancery aptly put it in *Guttman,* "[a] director cannot act loyally towards the corporation unless she acts in the good faith belief that her actions are in the corporation's best interest."[32]

We hold that *Caremark* articulates the necessary conditions predicate for director oversight liability: (a) the directors utterly failed to implement any reporting or information system or controls; *or* (b) having implemented such a system or controls, consciously failed to monitor or oversee its operations thus disabling themselves from being informed of risks or problems requiring their attention. In either case, imposition of liability requires a showing that the directors knew that they were not discharging their fiduciary obligations. Where

---

[29] That issue, whether a violation of the duty to act in good faith is a basis for the direct imposition of liability, was expressly left open in *Disney.* 906 A.2d at 67 n. 112. We address that issue here.

[30] *Guttman v. Huang,* 823 A.2d 492, 506 n. 34 (Del.Ch.2003).

[31] *See Cede & Co. v. Technicolor, Inc.,* 634 A.2d 345, 361 (Del.1993).

[32] *Guttman v. Huang,* 823 A.2d 492, 506 n. 34 (Del.Ch.2003).

directors fail to act in the face of a known duty to act, thereby demonstrating a conscious disregard for their responsibilities, they breach their duty of loyalty by failing to discharge that fiduciary obligation in good faith.

Chancery Court Decision

The plaintiffs contend that demand is excused under Rule 23.1 because AmSouth's directors breached their oversight duty and, as a result, face a "substantial likelihood of liability" as a result of their "utter failure" to act in good faith to put into place policies and procedures to ensure compliance with BSA and AML obligations. The Court of Chancery found that the plaintiffs did not plead the existence of "red flags"–"facts showing that the board ever was aware that AmSouth's internal controls were inadequate, that these inadequacies would result in illegal activity, and that the board chose to do nothing about problems it allegedly knew existed." In dismissing the derivative complaint in this action, the Court of Chancery concluded:

> This case is not about a board's failure to carefully consider a material corporate decision that was presented to the board. This is a case where information was not reaching the board because of ineffective internal controls With the benefit of hindsight, it is beyond question that AmSouth's internal controls with respect to the Bank Secrecy Act and anti-money laundering regulations compliance were inadequate. Neither party disputes that the lack of internal controls resulted in a huge fine–$50 million, alleged to be the largest ever of its kind. The fact of those losses, however, is not alone enough for a court to conclude that a majority of the corporation's board of directors is disqualified from considering demand that AmSouth bring suit against those responsible.

This Court reviews *de novo* a Court of Chancery's decision to dismiss a derivative suit under Rule 23.1.

Reasonable Reporting System Existed

The KPMG Report evaluated the various components of AmSouth's longstanding BSA/AML compliance program. The KPMG Report reflects that AmSouth's Board dedicated considerable resources to the BSA/AML compliance program and put into place numerous procedures and systems to attempt to ensure compliance. According to KPMG, the program's various components exhibited between a low and high degree of compliance with applicable laws and regulations.

The KPMG Report reflects that the directors not only discharged their oversight responsibility to establish an information and reporting system, but also proved that the system was designed to permit the directors to periodically monitor AmSouth's compliance with BSA and AML regulations. For example, as KPMG noted in 2004, AmSouth's designated BSA Officer "has made annual high-level presentations to the Board of Directors in each of the last five years." Further, the Board's Audit and Community Responsibility Committee (the "Audit Committee") oversaw AmSouth's BSA/AML compliance program on a quarterly basis. The KPMG Report states that "the BSA Officer presents BSA/AML training to the Board of Directors annually," and the "Corporate Security training is also presented to the Board of Directors."

The KPMG Report shows that AmSouth's Board at various times enacted written policies and procedures designed to ensure compliance with the BSA and AML regulations. For example, the Board adopted an amended bank-wide "BSA/AML Policy" on July 17, 2003–four months before AmSouth became aware that it was the target of a government investigation. Among other things, the July 17, 2003, BSA/AML Policy directs all AmSouth employees to immediately report suspicious transactions or activity to the BSA/AML Compliance Department or Corporate Security.

Complaint Properly Dismissed

In this case, the adequacy of the plaintiffs' assertion that demand is excused depends on whether the complaint alleges facts sufficient to show that the defendant *directors* are potentially personally liable for the failure of non-director bank *employees* to file SARs. Delaware courts have recognized that "[m]ost of the decisions that a corporation, acting through its human agents, makes are, of course, not the subject of director attention."[39] Consequently, a claim that directors are subject to personal liability for employee failures is "possibly the most difficult theory in corporation law upon which a plaintiff might hope to win a judgment."[40]

For the plaintiffs' derivative complaint to withstand a motion to dismiss, "only a sustained or systematic failure of the board to exercise oversight–such as an utter failure to attempt to assure a reasonable information and reporting system exists–will establish the lack of good faith that is a necessary condition to liability."[41] As the *Caremark* decision noted:

---

[39] *In re Caremark Int'l Inc. Deriv. Litig.*, 698 A.2d at 968.

[40] *Id.* at 967.

[41] *Id.* at 971.

Such a test of liability–lack of good faith as evidenced by sustained or systematic failure of a director to exercise reasonable oversight–is quite high. But, a demanding test of liability in the oversight context is probably beneficial to corporate shareholders as a class, as it is in the board decision context, since it makes board service by qualified persons more likely, while continuing to act as a stimulus to *good faith performance of duty* by such directors.[42]

The KPMG Report–which the plaintiffs explicitly incorporated by reference into their derivative complaint–refutes the assertion that the directors "never took the necessary steps...to ensure that a reasonable BSA compliance and reporting system existed." KPMG's findings reflect that the Board received and approved relevant policies and procedures, delegated to certain employees and departments the responsibility for filing SARs and monitoring compliance, and exercised oversight by relying on periodic reports from them. Although there ultimately may have been failures by employees to report deficiencies to the Board, there is no basis for an oversight claim seeking to hold the directors personally liable for such failures by the employees.

With the benefit of hindsight, the plaintiffs' complaint seeks to equate a bad outcome with bad faith. The lacuna in the plaintiffs' argument is a failure to recognize that the directors' good faith exercise of oversight responsibility may not invariably prevent employees from violating criminal laws, or from causing the corporation to incur significant financial liability, or both, as occurred in *Graham, Caremark* and this very case. In the absence of red flags, good faith in the context of oversight must be measured by the directors' actions to assure a reasonable information and reporting system exists and not by second-guessing after the occurrence of employee conduct that results in an unintended adverse outcome. Accordingly, we hold that the Court of Chancery properly applied *Caremark* and dismissed the plaintiffs' derivative complaint for failure to excuse demand by alleging particularized facts that created reason to doubt whether the directors had acted in good faith in exercising their oversight responsibilities.

Conclusion

The judgment of the Court of Chancery is affirmed.

---

[42] *Id.* (emphasis in original).

Notes and Questions

1. Notes

a. Chancellor Allen decided *Caremark*, and discussed a board's obligation to monitor, strictly as an aspect of the duty of care. That is, part of a board's duty to be informed is to ensure that appropriate monitoring systems are in place. In *Stone*, Justice Holland affirmed what had been generally assumed: *Caremark*, including the standard of review, governs the board's duty to monitor. However, he went on to say that *Caremark* liability "requires a showing that the directors knew that they were not discharging their fiduciary obligations." That's a significant change in *Caremark* jurisprudence.

A few Court of Chancery opinions suggested that the standard for finding liability under *Caremark* is so high that only intentional actions will suffice. That standard would transmute *Caremark* into a duty of loyalty claim. *Stone*, without any acknowledgment that it was choosing to redefine a *Caremark* claim from care to loyalty, did exactly that. *Stone* shifted the doctrinal emphasis in considering a duty to monitor from information gathering (duty of care) to the directors' intent (duty of loyalty).

b. Note the distinction between an obligation to follow up on information that comes to a director's attention that suggests the possibility of wrong-doing by the corporation or its agents and an obligation to establish, and monitor the efficacy of, a system of ensuring that sufficient information about the corporation is brought to the directors' attention.

c. The MBCA conceives of the duty of care as encompassing an obligation to oversee the corporation's actions, which is functionally similar to the obligation imposed in *Caremark*. *Compare* MBCA §§ 8.30 and 8.31(a), Official Comments.

2. Reality Check

a. What exactly was the court deciding? That is, what is the procedural posture of this case?

b. In what way were the directors of AmSouth alleged to have breached their duty of loyalty?

c. Why did the court find those allegations unconvincing?

d. Did the Supreme Court agree with the Court of Chancery in both reasoning and result?

3. Suppose

a. Suppose the directors knew that SARs were not being filed. Would that change the analysis or result?

b. Suppose the directors knew that SARs were not being filed and made a decision that the bank's likely profit from Hamric and Nance was greater than the bank's likely punishment if it were investigated. Would that change the analysis or result?

4. What Do You Think?

a. If monitoring is so important, and it is absolutely clear that the monitoring by the AmSouth board was inadequate, why is there no liability?

b. Chancellor Allen wrote that the standard for liability under *Caremark* "sustained or systematic failure of a director to exercise reasonable oversight – is quite high." Is it too high? Why should the standard not be gross negligence or even negligence? On these facts, would the directors be liable if the standard were either gross negligence or negligence?

c. Do you think directors should be able to deflect liability by demonstrating that they relied on others within the corporation? More specifically, should directors be able to avoid liability by demonstrating that they relied on information prepared at their specific request? That they relied on information prepared in the ordinary course of business? That they relied on those corporate officers and other corporate agents to whom the board has delegated authority? In this connection, the MBCA and DGCL provisions on directorial reliance are set out below.

5. You Draft It

a. Draft a statute that appropriately describes a director's ability to rely on the actions of others (including the ability to rely on information provided by others). The MBCA versions (current and pre-1998) and the DGCL are set out below:

MBCA Current § 8.30

> (c) In discharging board or committee duties a director, who does not have knowledge that makes reliance unwarranted, is entitled to rely on the performance by any of the persons specified in subsection (e)(1) or subsection (e)(3) to whom the board may have delegated, formally or informally by course of conduct, the authority

or duty to perform one or more of the board's functions that are delegable under applicable law.

(d) In discharging board or committee duties a director, who does not have knowledge that makes reliance unwarranted, is entitled to rely on information, opinions, reports or statements, including financial statements and other financial data, prepared or presented by any of the persons specified in subsection (e).

(e) A director is entitled to rely, in accordance with subsection (c) or (d), on:

> (1) one or more officers or employees of the corporation whom the director reasonably believes to be reliable and competent in the functions performed or the information, opinions, reports or statements provided;

> (2) legal counsel, public accountants, or other persons retained by the corporation as to matters involving skills or expertise the director reasonably believes are matters (i) within the particular person's professional or expert competence or (ii) as to which the particular person merits confidence; or

> (3) a committee of the board of directors of which the director is not a member if the director reasonably believes the committee merits confidence.

MBCA Pre-1998 § 8.30

In performing his duties, a director shall be entitled to rely on information, opinions, reports or statements, including financial statements and other financial data, in each case prepared or presented by:

> (a) One (1) or more officers or employees of the corporation whom the director reasonably believes to be reliable and competent in the matters presented,

> (b) Counsel, public accountants or other persons as to matters which the director reasonably believes to be within such person's professional or expert competence....

DGCL § 141(e)

A member of the board of directors, or a member of any committee designated by the board of directors, shall, in the performance of such member's duties, be fully protected in relying in good faith upon the records of the corporation and upon such information, opinions, reports or statements presented to the corporation by any of the corporation's officers or employees, or committees of the board of directors, or by any other person as to matters the member reasonably believes are within such other person's professional or expert competence and who has been selected with reasonable care by or on behalf of the corporation.

Page 400

Add the following case before "**4. Compensation of Directors and Senior Officers**":

Directors and officers move to different corporations with some regularity. They frequently stay within the same geographic location and continue to work within the same industry. These facts lead to a chronic corporate law issue: When is a director or officer no longer subject to fiduciary duties? The next case presents a typical situation.

Today Homes, Inc. v. Williams
634 S.E.2d 737 (Va. 2006)

Opinion by Justice G. STEVEN AGEE.

Today Homes, Inc., t/a Chesapeake Homes ("Chesapeake"), appeals the judgment of the Circuit Court of the City of Virginia Beach dismissing its amended bill of complaint against Emma Williams ... [and] George R. Woodhouse. For the reasons set forth below, we will affirm the judgment of the trial court in part, reverse the judgment in part, and remand for further proceedings.

I. FACTS AND MATERIAL PROCEEDINGS BELOW

Chesapeake is a property developer and builder of single-family homes. Like other companies in the home building industry, Chesapeake "needed land ... to build houses on." Williams served as Chesapeake's vice president of operations from June 2001 until March 13, 2003, and Woodhouse was Chesapeake's vice president of production during the same period. Williams and Woodhouse had a close working relationship and referred to themselves as "a team."

In the course of her employment, Williams was "responsible for all purchasing activities and customer service," but not the acquisition of land. Woodhouse supervised the actual construction work of the homes Chesapeake built. Neither person's job description involved finding or purchasing lots for building.

At the beginning of 2003, Frank Grossman, a realtor with Long & Foster Realtors, told Woodhouse about certain property he had listed for sale in Hampton ("the Sinclair Property"). Woodhouse mentioned the Sinclair Property to Williams and showed her a site plan. At that time, the development plan for the Sinclair Property included a "55 and older active adult communit[y]." Woodhouse testified that he did not believe Chesapeake would be interested in the property because Chesapeake "didn't do any 55 and older active adult communities." Williams also believed Chesapeake would not be interested in purchasing the property. Williams and Woodhouse had no further discussions about the property until after Chesapeake terminated Williams' employment on March 13, 2003 [2]

Williams testified without contradiction that prior to her termination, she had no intention of leaving Chesapeake and starting her own housing development company, and she had not identified any building sites for purchase.

Woodhouse prepared a letter resigning from his employment with Chesapeake the day Williams was terminated, but did not submit the letter until April 24, 2003, when he gave his two weeks' notice. Woodhouse did no further work for Chesapeake after May 9 ....

After Williams' termination, but while Woodhouse remained employed by Chesapeake, the two discussed going into business together and caused Majestic to be incorporated on March 27, 2003. Williams and Woodhouse were listed as president and secretary, respectively, of Majestic. Woodhouse began working for Majestic on May 15, 2003, and drew his first paycheck on June 1, 2003.

After forming Majestic, Williams searched for properties to purchase by contacting real estate companies, including Long & Foster. Near the end of March 2003, Woodhouse put Grossman in contact with Williams, and discussed the Sinclair Property with her. When Grossman showed Williams the Sinclair Property, she recognized it as "the same property that [she] had heard about from [Woodhouse]" earlier in the year when she was working for Chesapeake.

On April 15, 2003, Majestic entered into a contract ... to purchase ... the Sinclair Property. In 2004, Majestic had gross profit from the sale of homes on the Sinclair Property of $4,469,585.00. There is no dispute that neither Williams nor Woodhouse ever disclosed the Sinclair Property to Chesapeake or received Chesapeake's consent to acquire it.

Chesapeake filed [an] amended bill of complaint alleging Williams and Woodhouse, as corporate officers of Chesapeake, breached their common law and contractual fiduciary duty to Chesapeake when they failed to disclose the existence of the Sinclair Property to Chesapeake and later purchased it themselves through Majestic.

---

[2] The termination of Williams' employment by Chesapeake is not at issue in this appeal.

After a one-day bench trial, the trial court dismissed Chesapeake's amended bill of complaint and entered a final decree on September 27, 2005, stating that Chesapeake "failed to meet its burden of proof as to all counts contained in the Amended Bill of Complaint." [T]he trial court determined that Chesapeake had not proven that Williams and Woodhouse breached their fiduciary duty to Chesapeake. We granted Chesapeake this appeal.

Chesapeake makes ten assignments of error, which can be condensed to the following ... issues: (1) the trial court erred in finding that Williams and Woodhouse (collectively "the Defendants") did not breach a fiduciary duty to Chesapeake when they failed to disclose the existence of the Sinclair Property to Chesapeake while one or both was still employed by Chesapeake, and later purchased the property through Majestic; [and (2)] the trial court misallocated the burden of proof by placing upon Chesapeake the burden of showing the breach of fiduciary duty rather than requiring the Defendants to show that they did not breach their fiduciary obligations ....

II. ANALYSIS

[T]he Defendants argue they learned of the Sinclair Property in their individual capacities, and not in their role as officers of Chesapeake. Thus, they argue there was no duty of disclosure on their part and no corresponding breach of fiduciary duty.

No reasonable reading of the trial court's determination could lead to a conclusion other than that it found the Sinclair Property to be a corporate opportunity for Chesapeake. The unchallenged finding of the trial court is now the law of the case and binding on the parties for purposes of appeal.

The Defendants do not contest on appeal that they were officers of Chesapeake, and in that capacity, had a fiduciary relationship to Chesapeake. Neither is there any dispute that Woodhouse or Williams did not disclose the Sinclair Property to Chesapeake or seek Chesapeake's consent to take the Sinclair Property.

Our inquiry now turns to what duty, if any, the Defendants owed Chesapeake regarding the Sinclair Property. It is a fundamental principle that a corporate officer or director is under a fiduciary obligation not to divert a corporate business opportunity for personal gain because the opportunity is considered the property of the corporation.

The unbending rule that a fiduciary entrusted with the business of another cannot be allowed to make that business an object of interest to himself, is abrogated if the fiduciary obtains the consent of the corporation after full disclosure. The motive of self-interest is so natural and the danger of temptation to secure private advantage so great, that good faith alone is not sufficient in the absence of full disclosure and consent of the interested parties to make an exception to the general rule that a corporate fiduciary cannot enter into any relation or do any act inconsistent with the interest of the corporation.

The Defendants argue that this requirement of "full disclosure" is an unworkable burden on a corporation's officers because it "require[s] corporate officers to disclose all business opportunities of which they learn ... regardless of whether the corporate officer is planning to take advantage of the opportunity personally." This view misconstrues the requirements of disclosure, which become operative and relevant only when an officer receiving information about a potential corporate opportunity then appropriates that opportunity for his own use. Thus, an officer's desire to take an opportunity as his own, puts him on notice of his fiduciary duty to disclose the opportunity to the corporation before acting upon it for his personal benefit.

The trial court found that "[t]he information [Woodhouse] received [regarding the Sinclair Property] did not become important until ... March 13," the day Williams' employment with Chesapeake was terminated and Woodhouse first alerted [Chesapeake] of his intention to resign. That factual finding by the trial court was not the subject of an assignment of error or cross-error and is now the law of the case. The Defendants' casual knowledge of the Sinclair Property's existence in early 2003 is not, by itself, a basis for requiring disclosure or attaching liability for any of their later actions.

We must initially address, however, Chesapeake's contention that the trial court "misallocated the burden of proof, putting on Chesapeake Homes the burden of showing breach of fiduciary duty rather than requiring Williams and Woodhouse to show that they did not breach their fiduciary obligations." We agree with Chesapeake that the trial court erred in this regard.

Once a plaintiff has shown that a corporate opportunity existed and the corporate fiduciary appropriated it without disclosure and the consent of the corporation, a *prima facie* case has been shown. Under our jurisprudence, the burden shifts to the defendant fiduciary to show why the taking of the corporate opportunity was not a breach of his fiduciary duty.

The trial court's finding that neither Williams nor Woodhouse breached a fiduciary duty to Chesapeake was thus based on the wrong rule of law as it incorrectly placed the burden of proof on Chesapeake. Accordingly, we will reverse the trial court's judgment and remand the case to the trial court for a determination of whether there was a breach of fiduciary duty upon proper application of the burden of proof. However, we will reverse and remand only with respect to Woodhouse because the record is uncontradicted as to Williams regardless of the burden of proof. Even though the trial court erred in allocating to Chesapeake the burden of showing Williams' breach of fiduciary duty, it is clear on this record there could be no breach by Williams.

Chesapeake argues that Williams' fiduciary duty to Chesapeake continued following her termination on March 13 and that her purchase of the Sinclair Property was in violation of that duty. It is true that resignation or termination does not automatically free a director or employee from his or her fiduciary obligations. Liability post-termination continues only for those transactions completed after termination of the officer's association with the corporation, but which began during the existence of the relationship or that were founded on information gained during the relationship. Whether specific conduct taken prior to resignation breaches a fiduciary duty requires a case by case analysis.

The record for purposes of appeal establishes that Williams' purchase of the Sinclair Property through Majestic was not "founded on information gained during" her employment with Chesapeake. Prior to her termination, Williams had no intention of leaving Chesapeake and starting her own development company. There is no evidence in the record that she used any of Chesapeake's resources to establish Majestic or regarding the Sinclair Property. Williams' casual knowledge of the Sinclair Property before her termination triggered no duty to disclose because her relationship with the Sinclair Property as a corporate opportunity occurred only after March 13th. After March 13th, Williams was under no fiduciary duty to Chesapeake because she was no longer an officer.[6]

There was thus no basis for liability on Williams' part after March 13 for breach of a fiduciary duty to Chesapeake as she had no duty. Thus, even though it applied the wrong burden of proof, the trial court did not err in dismissing the amended bill of complaint as to Williams.

III. CONCLUSION

For the foregoing reasons, we will reverse the trial court's judgment dismissing the amended bill of complaint as to Woodhouse and affirm the trial court's judgment as to Williams .... We will remand the case to the trial court for further proceedings to determine whether Woodhouse breached a fiduciary duty to Chesapeake, in conformance with the principles expressed in this opinion.

Notes and Questions

1. Reality Check

a. Why did the court find that Ms. Williams could not be liable?

b. Why did the court find that Mr. Woodhouse might be liable?

---

[6] In contrast to Williams, Woodhouse did continue as an officer of Chesapeake for at least two months after March 13th and took certain actions in regard to the Sinclair Property.

2. Suppose

a. If Ms. Williams had been responsible for acquiring land while she was at Chesapeake, would the court's reasoning or the result have been different?

3. What Do You Think?

a. Were Ms. Williams and Mr. Woodhouse differently situated?

b. Do you think the fact that Ms. Williams' duties did not include acquiring land on behalf of Chesapeake should make a difference?

c. Do you think the disclosure requirement imposed by the court is workable? If so, is it wise? If not, what disclosure rule would you impose?

Page 400

Add the following case at the end of the section titled "**4. Compensation of Directors and Senior Officers**":

Desimone v. Barrows

– A.2d –, 2007 WL 1670255 (Del. Ch.)

STRINE, Vice Chancellor.

I. *Introduction*

The nominal defendant in this derivative action, Sycamore Networks, Inc., is one of the many corporations drawing adverse attention regarding the methods by which it granted stock options to its officers, employees, and directors. Last year, the Securities and Exchange Commission and United States Department of Justice launched investigations into Sycamore's stock options practices on the suspicion that Sycamore had misrepresented–by backdating–certain options grants and engaged in related misbehavior.

Armed with the fact of the government investigations into Sycamore, with generic facts about options backdating gleaned from newspaper articles, and with allegations contained in (and a so-called "smoking gun" internal memorandum (the "Internal Memo") attached to) a complaint filed by a disgruntled former Sycamore executive in another court, the plaintiff, John S. Desimone, filed a complaint in this court on June 9, 2006 without making a demand on Sycamore's board and without having sought to obtain books and records under [DGCL] § 220. The centerpiece of Desimone's complaint is the Internal Memo, written by an unknown author, which suggests that options granted to six rank-and-file employees in late 2000 were altered to have the option grant date coincide with the date of the lowest trading price of Sycamore's stock during the preceding quarter. When that Memo was revealed to Sycamore's board of directors in early 2005, Sycamore's Audit Committee launched an internal investigation. After that investigation, Sycamore disclosed that it had improperly accounted for certain stock option grants and restated its earnings for the fiscal years 2000-2003.

Desimone seeks to bring claims on behalf of Sycamore against the recipients of the allegedly improper grants and against Sycamore's board for breaching their fiduciary duties by allowing the grants to occur. The defendants have moved to dismiss the complaint for lack of standing, for failure to adequately plead demand excusal under Court of Chancery Rule 23.1 and for failure to state a claim under Rule 12(b)(6). In this opinion, I conclude that the motion must be granted.

For starters, plaintiff Desimone has only held stock in Sycamore since February 2002 and lacks standing under [DGCL] § 327 to pursue the lion's share of the claims he asserts, most of which are based on options grants that occurred in 2000 and 2001. Therefore, consistent with long-standing precedent such as *Elster v. American Airlines*,[1] and this court's recent decision in *Ryan v. Gifford*,[2] addressing an identical situation in the same manner, I hold that Desimone is barred by § 327 from attacking the options grants made before he became a Sycamore stockholder.

I also find that the defendants' Rule 23.1 and 12(b)(6) arguments dispose of Desimone's challenges to all of the stock option grants. Desimone challenges a number of different types of options grants and in determining the viability of Desimone's claims, it is useful to categorize his claims by the type of grant at issue. The first two categories involve grants of options to Sycamore's rank-and-file employees and to its officers (the "Employee Grants" and "Officer Grants," respectively). The last category involves grants of options to Sycamore's outside directors (the "Outside Director Grants"). The analysis appropriate to address the first two categories is, I find, different from that appropriate to address the third.

As Desimone concedes, the question of whether he has satisfied his burden under Rule 23.1 must be answered by applying the test set forth in *Rales v. Blasband*[3] because Desimone does not challenge a business decision made by the Sycamore board. As a result, the relevant inquiry is whether the Sycamore board, as constituted at the time Desimone brought suit, could exercise an independent and disinterested business judgment in responding to a demand

---

[1] 100 A.2d 219 (Del. Ch.1953).

[2] 918 A.2d 341 (Del. Ch.2007).

[3] 634 A.2d 927 (Del.1993).

regarding Desimone's claims.[4] Because neither of the two members of the Sycamore board who were both officers and employees received any of the Employee or Officer Grants that Desimone challenges, the key issue under *Rales* as to the Employee and Officer Grants is whether, assuming the pled facts to be true, a majority of the Sycamore board faces a substantial likelihood of personal liability as a result of those Grants, thus compromising their ability to consider a demand impartially.[5]

II. *General Background*

As has been discussed, plaintiff Desimone challenges three different categories of options grants: Employee Grants, Officer Grants, and Outside Director Grants. This section of the opinion will outline the general background relevant to analyzing all of the categories in contest. Then, the opinion will address the merits of the defendants' dismissal arguments, setting forth the more specific facts as to each category in the course of analyzing the viability of Desimone's claims.

Before doing so, it is helpful to define some of the new jargon that has entered the corporation law lexicon as a result of the ongoing stock option controversy. Stock options "backdating" is a practice whereby a public company issues options on a particular date while falsely recording that the options were issued on an earlier date when the company's stock was trading at a lower price. The options are purportedly issued with an exercise price equal to the market price on the date of the option grant. But, in fact, because the grant dates were falsified, the options were "in the money" when granted. The practice of "spring loading" stock options involves making market-value options grants at a time when the company possesses, but has not yet released, favorable, material non-public information that will likely increase the stock price when disclosed. Conversely, "bullet-dodging" options are granted just after the company releases negative information to the market thereby allowing the recipient the benefit of a lower exercise price that reflects the price decline caused by the negative information.

A. *Sycamore's Business and Board*

Sycamore develops and markets optical networking products. It was founded in 1998 and went public at the height of the tech boom in 1999. Since going public,

---

[4] *Id.* at 934; *Guttman v. Huang,* 823 A.2d 492, 501-03 (Del. Ch.2003).

[5] *Rales,* 634 A.2d at 934; *Guttman,* 823 A.2d at 500; *In re Baxter International, Inc. S'holders Litig.,* 654 A.2d 1268, 1270-71 (Del. Ch.1995).

Sycamore's share price has fluctuated widely. The initial public offering was at $38 per share. From there, the stock went up to a high of more than $165 apiece in August 2000. By 2001, its shares were trading below $10 and currently trade between $3 and $4.

Two of Sycamore's founders serve on its six-member board. They are defendants Gururaj Deshpande, who serves as Chairman of the Board, and Daniel Smith, who serves as Chief Executive Officer and President. Deshpande owns 16.5% of the corporation's shares. He does not receive any compensation, other than reimbursement of expenses, to be Chairman of the Board. Smith owns 15.5% of the corporation's shares. He receives an annual $100,000 salary to be CEO and President and has not received any bonus or stock option grant in any year since Sycamore went public.

Notably, neither Deshpande nor Smith received any of the options disputed in this case. In fact, neither of them own options in Sycamore. They simply own, between them, nearly a third of the corporation's common stock.

The other four Sycamore directors (the "Outside Directors") are directors who would, plaintiff Desimone must concede, be deemed independent for all purposes, save in situations when they have a personal interest at stake. The four Outside Directors are defendants Timothy Barrows, Paul Chisholm, Paul Ferri, and John Gerdelman. Their only compensation for board service is their receipt of stock options under a stockholder-approved option plan. All of the "Director Defendants" have served on Sycamore's board since 1998, except for defendant Chisholm, who joined the board in 2002.

Desimone's demand excusal arguments stress two of Sycamore's board committees, the Compensation Committee and the Audit Committee. At all relevant times, the Compensation Committee consisted of two board members, defendants Barrows and Ferri. At various times, each of defendants Barrows, Ferri, Chisholm, and Gerdelman has served on the three-member Audit Committee.

The complaint also names as defendants five of Sycamore's executive officers. Each of the "Officer Defendants" is alleged to have received one or more backdated options grant. The complaint focuses in particular on one of the Officer Defendants, Frances Jewels. Jewels was Sycamore's Chief Financial Officer, Treasurer, Secretary, and Vice President of Finance and Administration from 1999 until her resignation effective October 5, 2004. She is alleged to have been the "enforcer" and overseer of the illicit plan to backdate the Employee Grants.

B. *Sycamore's Stockholder-Approved Option Plans*

All of the challenged stock options grants were issued under authority of one of two stockholder-approved stock option plans: a Non-Employee Director Stock

Option Plan (the "Outside Director Plan") and a Stock Incentive Plan (the "Incentive Plan").

The Outside Director Plan automatically granted 30,000 options to each of Sycamore's Outside Directors each year on the date of Sycamore's annual stockholders meeting. The Outside Director Plan also required that the exercise price of those options be equal to 100% of the fair market value of Sycamore's stock on the date of the grant. The options granted under the Outside Director Plan were immediately exercisable, but were subject to a three year vesting schedule that prevented the recipients from realizing any immediate value from the options. Under the schedule, a third of the options vested after one year, another third after two years, and the last third three years from the date of the grant. Until the options vested, the recipient was effectively prevented from selling or attempting to borrow against any shares acquired by exercising the options.

The terms of the Incentive Plan, under which all of the challenged Officer and Employee Grants were made, has more moving parts and therefore demands a bit more description. The first important aspect of the Incentive Plan involves who was charged with administering it. The Incentive Plan states that "[t]he Plan will be administered by a committee or committees appointed by the Board of Directors of the Company ... and consisting of two or more members of the Board." Importantly, it also provides:

> To the extent permitted by applicable law, the Board may delegate to one or more executive officers of the Company the power to grant Stock Rights and exercise such other powers under the Plan as the Board may determine, provided that the Board shall fix the maximum number of shares subject to Stock Rights and the maximum number of shares for any one participant to be made by such executive officers.

In other words, with few limitations, the Incentive Plan contemplated that Sycamore's directors themselves might have a very limited role in making certain options grants by permitting the board to delegate its authority under the Plan to Sycamore's executive officers. The complaint alleges no facts regarding how Sycamore implemented the Incentive Plan, who was charged with administering it, and whether, and to which, executive officers the board delegated any option-granting responsibilities.

Importantly, the Incentive Plan differs from the Outside Director Plan in that it does not require that all options grants be priced at fair market value on the date of the grant. Rather, the Incentive Plan merely states that the exercise price per share will be set at the discretion of those charged with administering the Plan. To be clear that the Incentive Plan contemplated issuance of non-fair-market-value options, the options pricing section of the Plan contains a carve-out requiring only that options intended to qualify as incentive stock options under § 422(b) of the Internal Revenue Code or as performance-based compensation under § 162(m) of the Internal Revenue Code be priced at no less than 100% of fair market value on the option grant date.[22] Although the complaint alleges that both Plans, the Outside Director Plan and the Incentive Plan, required options to be priced at fair market value on the date of grant, the clear language of the Incentive Plan contradicts that allegation.[23]

[T]he complaint fairly implies that Sycamore accounted for all of the Employee and Officer Grants issued under the Incentive Plan as having been priced at fair market value on the date of grant, and having led stockholders, the market more generally, the recipients, and securities and tax regulatory authorities to believe that the favorable accounting[24] and tax treatment available for fair-market-value-based grants applied to the Grants now under attack.

The Incentive Plan also differs from the Outside Director Plan in that it gives Sycamore's Compensation Committee discretion to set the vesting schedule for any grants made under the Incentive Plan. Plaintiff Desimone has alleged, however, that all of the Employee and Officer Grants were made with a three year vesting schedule in which the shares vested in equal quarterly installments. As was the case with the Outside Director Plan, recipients of Grants under the Incentive Plan were precluded from realizing any immediate value from unvested options because any shares acquired by exercising unvested options were subject to a repurchase right in favor of Sycamore at the option exercise price.

---

[22] Sections 422(b) and 162(m) of the Internal Revenue Code, 26 U.S.C. §§ 422(b) & 162(m), condition the favorable income tax treatment for certain types of stock options on several prerequisites, one of which is that the options be priced at no less than fair market value on the date of the grant. Section 422(b) permits the recipient of a qualifying option grant to recognize no income as a result of the grant if the corporation does not take a deduction attributable to it. Under § 162(m), performance-based compensation, which can include certain market-price stock options, is exempt from the otherwise applicable rule that an employer cannot deduct compensation to any single employee in excess of $1 million.

[23] *See In re Wheelabrator Tech's, Inc. S'holders Litig.*, 1992 WL 212595, at *3 (Del.Ch.1992) ("The Court is hardly bound to accept as true a demonstrable mischaracterization and the erroneous allegations that flow from it."); *see also Malpiede v. Townson*, 780 A.2d 1075, 1083 (Del.2001) ("A claim may be dismissed if allegations in the complaint or in the exhibits incorporated into the complaint effectively negate the claim as a matter of law.").

[24] Under generally accepted accounting principles ("GAAP") prevailing during the time of the Grants challenged in the complaint, a corporation did not have to recognize any compensation expense associated with grants of stock options when the exercise price of the options was equal to or greater than the fair market value of the company's stock on the date of the grant. By contrast, when a company granted options with a below-market exercise price, it was required to recognize a non-cash expense in the amount of the difference.

C. *The Revelation of Sycamore's Backdating Scheme*

Sycamore's options practices became controversial when Sycamore's former Director of Human Resources, Stephen Landry, publicly accused Sycamore of backdating options. Having foregone any effort to obtain books and records using his statutory right of access, plaintiff Desimone largely bases his complaint on Landry's accusations and other public documents.

Because Desimone depends so heavily on Landry, a recitation of Landry's contentions is unavoidable. Sycamore hired Landry in October 1999 and allegedly "eased him out" of the company in the fall of 2000. Upon his exit, Landry entered into a severance agreement with Sycamore, which he negotiated with defendant Francis Jewels, Sycamore's then-CFO. That severance agreement granted Landry a number of stock options. When Sycamore's stock price declined sharply in the following years, those options went underwater and Landry's severance package became worthless.

In late 2004, after Jewels had left Sycamore's employ, Landry wrote a letter to defendant Deshpande, Sycamore's Chairman, hoping to renegotiate the severance agreement. Landry succeeded in getting a meeting with Sycamore's new CFO and tried to use his knowledge of Sycamore's options backdating practices as leverage. Landry told a story in which Jewels was the boss and he was an underling in a conspiracy to backdate options grants. Jewels allegedly instructed Landry repeatedly to alter and falsify human resources documents in order to corroborate falsified options grant dates. Often, this was accomplished by forging personnel file documents to change a newly-hired employee's start date to correspond to the date on which Jewels had determined to backdate the Employee Grant

In early 2005, Landry presented Sycamore with the Internal Memo, penned by an unknown author in early 2001, that discusses the fact that options granted to six Sycamore employees were either deliberately altered to reflect a grant date of December 21, 2000, the date on which the stock price hit its low for the quarter, or were cancelled and reissued with a December 21, 2000 effective date. Sycamore's stock price on December 21, 2000 was $29.125, down from $56.94 ten days earlier. Within the next twenty days, the stock price increased 76.4% to $51.38. According to the complaint, the manipulation of grant dates allowed the employees receiving options to reap a substantial and instant paper gain. But, as Desimone concedes, the options were subject to a three-year vesting schedule, and could not be used as collateral, precluding immediate realization of that gain.[28]

---

[28] In fact, according to the complaint, by early April 2001, just over three months after the December 2000 Grants, Sycamore's stock price was trading below $10 per share and has never recovered to the price it was at on December 21, 2000. By the time the first installment of the December 21, 2000 Grants vested, they were underwater and have never gotten back into the money. Given that Sycamore's stock is currently trading between $3 and $4 per share, in order for the recipients of the

The Internal Memo separately discusses each of the six employees' options and suggests various courses of action designed to cover up the fact that the grant dates were being manipulated. Substantial covert actions were detailed to avoid having the backdating operation detected,[29] and the Memo makes a "risk assessment" for the actions taken with respect to each employee. The Memo considered many of the cover-up actions to be "low risk." For example, for one of the employees, the Memo states,

> She is a rank and file employee and the Company has no prior experience with her (although she does have a relationship with [another Sycamore employee] that could work to our advantage should the risk of exposure on this agreement surface). Low audit risk (exposure on payroll registers and on the medical insurance effective dates, both of which will remain unchanged, however, the auditors never reference these documents in their audits).

For others, the risk was higher: "There is an audit risk since the grant was originally issued in Q1 and the cancellation occurred after the Q1 audit. Q1 options will not balance to audit records and diluted shares outstanding for Q1 will not balance."

Upon learning of the Internal Memo, Sycamore's Audit Committee launched an investigation into Sycamore's historic accounting for stock options grants. That investigation revealed a number of options grants between 1999 and 2001 that were incorrectly accounted for under GAAP. According to Sycamore's recent public disclosures, the improperly-accounted-for grants included six new employee options grants in which employment start date records were deliberately modified to provide lower exercise prices and six existing stock options grants that were deliberately cancelled and reissued to provide for lower exercise prices. The investigation also revealed an issue regarding a grant of options to several employees purportedly made on April 14, 2000, "where, from a review of supporting records, it appeared that the number of options granted likely was not ultimately determined until April 26, 2000." In other words, the options were granted on April 26, 2000, but backdated to April 14. April 14, 2000, like December 21, 2000, was allegedly an auspicious grant date. Sycamore's stock price was $59, down from $129 ten days earlier. Within the next twenty days, the stock price increased 45% to over $74. Again, Desimone claims that this means that the options recipients immediately made a

---

December 2000 Grants to realize any value from their options, Sycamore's stock price must increase nearly 1000% before the options expire in December 2010.

[29] For example, with respect to a newly hired employee in Sycamore's legal department whose option grant date was manipulated, the Internal Memo states: "Requires new offer letter for the file to adjust the salary difference from her actual date of hire 11/27/00 and 12/21/00. Adjustment will be addressed in the offer letter in the form of a sign on bonus."

$15 per share profit. But the vesting and other restrictions applicable to the Grants precluded the recipients from realizing it.

As a result of the investigation, Sycamore restated its earnings for fiscal years 2000-2003. The reason for the restatement was that the corporation had accounted for a large number of options as having been granted at fair market value on the date of the grant when in fact they had been granted at a later date than was reported, a later date when the fair market value of the corporation's shares was higher than the reported grant date. When accurately accounted for, these "in the money grants" had to be reflected as a non-cash charge on the company's balance sheet, thus reducing the earnings previously reported. In sum, with the bulk of the adjustment applied to fiscal year 2001, Sycamore took an additional $29.9 million non-cash charge. At the conclusion of the initial stage of the investigation, Sycamore did not penalize any officer, director, or employee, and no option recipient lost her option grant, although it appears some have agreed to re-price some of their options.

III. *The Defendants' Dismissal Arguments*

Three major arguments for dismissal are advanced by the Director Defendants. First, the Director Defendants argue that Desimone lacks standing under [DGCL] § 327 to challenge most of the option Grants because he did not become a Sycamore stockholder until after they were made. Second, the Director Defendants contend that Desimone's derivative claims must be dismissed because he did not make a demand on Sycamore's board and has failed to plead demand excusal with the particularity required by Court of Chancery Rule 23.1. Third, the Director Defendants argue that Desimone's allegations fail to state a claim under Rule 12(b)(6). I address these arguments in turn, beginning with the Director Defendants' standing argument.

IV. *Desimone Lacks Standing To Challenge The Pre-2002 Options Grants*

Section 327 of the Delaware General Corporation Law requires that a derivative plaintiff have been "a stockholder of the corporation at the time of the transaction of which [he] complains." The complaint alleges that Desimone has owned 700 shares of Sycamore common stock since February 4, 2002. Desimone concedes that all but two of the allegedly improper options Grants were made before he became a stockholder. The only Grants that occurred after Desimone acquired his stock were a set of Officer Grants that occurred in April 2002 and a set of Outside Director Grants in December 2003.

Therefore, because Desimone did not buy Sycamore stock until February 2002, he lacks standing to challenge all of the options Grants that occurred before he became a Sycamore stockholder.

V. *The Complaint's Allegations About Sycamore's Stock Options Practices*

Because Desimone does have standing to challenge two of the options Grants identified in the complaint, I cannot avoid addressing those Grants. Because I have to do that anyway, in the interests of efficiency, I evaluate more generally whether the entire complaint must be dismissed under either Rule 23.1 for failure to make a demand or Rule 12(b)(6) for failure to state a claim. [I] turn to the substantive issues raised by Desimone's allegations.

B. *Options Backdating Under Delaware Law*

This court recently had occasion to consider issues similar to the ones presented here in its carefully-reasoned and well-written decisions, *Ryan v. Gifford*[70] and *In re Tyson Foods, Inc. Consol. S'holders Litig.*[71] Therefore, before engaging in an analysis of the challenged Grants, a brief discussion of those cases is in order.

In *Ryan,* Chancellor Chandler held that when a stockholder-approved stock option plan requires all options to be granted with current market exercise prices, a director acts disloyally by knowingly approving backdated options. As the Chancellor explained, representing to the company's shareholders, the public markets, and regulatory authorities that an option grant was given at fair market value on the date of the grant when in fact the option was backdated to an earlier time when the stock price was lower, involves a "fundamental, incontrovertible lie." In that regard, the Chancellor noted that "it is difficult to conceive of a context in which a director may simultaneously lie to his shareholders ... and yet satisfy his duty of loyalty."

In *Ryan,* the plaintiff alleged that a three-member compensation committee, which amounted to half of the six-member board, knowingly backdated the option grants at issue and that a fourth director was interested in the option grants because he was the one who received them and did so knowing that they were backdated. The Chancellor thus applied the *Aronson* standard for demand excusal and held that demand was excused because at least half of the board participated in the decision to backdate options and that a knowing violation of a stockholder-approved option plan was not a valid exercise of business judgment. Alternatively, the Chancellor held that demand would also be excused under the *Rales* standard because the directors who knowingly approved or received backdated options grants faced a substantial likelihood of personal liability for breaching their fiduciary duty of loyalty.

---

[70] 918 A.2d 341 (Del. Ch.2007).

[71] 919 A.2d 563 (Del. Ch.2007).

Tyson considered a different issue. In that case, the directors were not alleged to have backdated any option grants, but rather to have engaged in "spring loading." The allegation in *Tyson* was that the directors engaged in a pattern of behavior over a number of years whereby just before the company would issue a positive announcement that was likely to cause an increase in the company's stock price, a large discretionary award of stock options would be issued to key insiders, including several of the directors. Also critical was the allegation that the stock option plan in *Tyson* required all option grants to be issued at fair market value. Based on those pled facts, the Chancellor held that the plaintiffs stated a breach of fiduciary duty claim against the directors who approved and who received the spring-loaded options. In so holding, the Chancellor noted that the plaintiffs had pled a very specific set of facts that satisfied the following requirements he articulated for premising a claim on spring loading: "First, a plaintiff must allege that options were issued according to a stockholder-approved employee compensation plan. Second, a plaintiff must allege that the directors that approved spring-loaded (or bullet-dodging) options (a) possessed material non-public information soon to be released that would impact the company's share price, and (b) issued those options with the intent to circumvent otherwise valid stockholder-approved restrictions upon the exercise price of options."

As I understand it, the plaintiffs pled in *Tyson* that the option plan was sold to stockholders on the basis that options would be granted *not* as a reward for *past* performance, but *only* to give incentives for recipients to work hard and well in the *future*. By allegedly using the plan as an undisclosed means to grant large discretionary bonuses, the *Tyson* defendants were accused of manipulative, secretive behavior at odds with the rationale for the plan–a rationale the stockholders were told by the defendants themselves. The Chancellor held that conduct of that precise kind raised, for pleading purposes, a claim for breach of fiduciary duty.[80]

In *Tyson,* demand was excused because the plaintiff pled with particularity facts to establish a reasonable doubt that the company's board as a whole was capable of acting independently of the individuals who knowingly received the spring-loaded options grants. As a result, the entire board was compromised in its ability to disinterestedly consider a demand challenging those grants.

---

[80] One could also read *Tyson* as holding that the defendants consciously caused the corporation to breach the implied covenant of good faith and fair dealing in the option plan. By making an intentional decision to award a discretionary option grant before announcing positive news they already possessed but that the markets did not, the defendants could be seen as exploiting an interstitial gap in a manner that clearly deprived the stockholders of the bargain they thought they had made. As I note a bit later, the fiduciary duty tool was necessary to employ to hold the non-recipient directors responsible for any harm created.

C. *Proceed with Care: The Legal Complexities Raised by Various Options Practices*

As in *Ryan* and *Tyson,* issues of backdating and spring loading are presented here. But there are some very important differences between the allegations made here about the Employee, Officer, and Outside Director Grants, and those that were made in *Ryan* and *Tyson.* The first is that the Incentive Plan, the stockholder-approved option plan under which all of the Employee and Officer Grants were made, did not by its terms require that all options be priced at fair market value on the date of the grant. Rather, the Incentive Plan gave Sycamore's directors discretion to set the exercise price of the options and expressly permitted below-market-value options to be granted. This case thus presents a different question than those involved in *Ryan* and *Tyson,* which is whether corporate officials breach their fiduciary duties when they, despite having express permission under a stockholder-approved option plan to grant below-market options, represent to shareholders, markets, and regulatory authorities that they are granting fair-market-value options when in fact they are secretly manipulating the exercise price of the option.

As to that question, there is also the subsidiary question of whether the means matters. For example, do backdating and spring loading always have the same implications? In this respect, the contraventions of stockholder-approved option plans that allegedly occurred in *Ryan* and *Tyson* are not the only cause for concern. The tax and accounting fraud that flows from acts of concealed options backdating involve clear violations of positive law. But even in such cases, there are important nuances about *who* bears responsibility when the corporation violates the law, nuances that turn importantly on the state of mind of those accused of involvement.

That point highlights the second important difference between this case and *Ryan* and *Tyson.* In contrast to the plaintiff in *Ryan,* plaintiff Desimone has pled no facts to suggest even the hint of a culpable state of mind on the part of any director. Likewise, Desimone has not, as was done in *Tyson,* pled any facts to suggest that any director was incapable of acting independently of the recipients of any of the Employee or Officer Grants. The absence of pled facts of these kinds underscores the utility of a cautious, non-generic approach to addressing the various options practices now under challenge in many lawsuits. The various practices have jurisprudential implications that are also diverse, not identical, and the policy purposes of different bodies of related law (corporate, securities, and tax) could be lost if courts do not proceed with prudence. Indeed, within the corporate law alone, there are subtle issues raised by options practices.

By way of example, consider the concerns of some distinguished scholars about the boundaries between law and equity in this area. Those scholars posit that if directors violate the express terms of a stockholder-approved stock option plan, they have acted without authority and their actions may be set aside as invalid, because the directors did not have the authority to take those actions in the first place.[82] Therefore, these scholars see little room for the application of fiduciary principles to judge such behavior.[83] Underlying this fear, or so I perceive, is the justified concern that concepts of fiduciary duty not be used in an unprincipled and wholly-elastic way to reach any and all behavior that, upon first blush, strikes judges as inappropriate.

These scholars' concern about analytical rigor of this kind is one I embrace. But the common law of corporations cannot and should not fail to consider the fiduciary consequences of director behavior that involves a breach of contract or violation of law. In fact, I harbor that belief for reasons consistent with these scholars' concerns, particularly their concern that directors might otherwise be too lightly subjected to liability in situations involving alleged failures in exercising due care. Although the reasons for that belief cannot be set forth in full here, an example might illustrate why the rigorous application of legal and equitable concepts to the same transaction might be required to render the most just decision.

Assume a situation when a corporation, whose charter has an exculpatory provision authorized by [DGCL] § 102(b)(7), has consistently backdated options in violation of a stockholder-approved option plan. The backdating was concealed from stockholders through false accounting. But the option grants were to highly-educated researchers, none of whom were involved in the decision-making process regarding the grants of options. As is often the case with illegal schemes, this one was exposed. The corporation has had to restate its earnings, deal with tax authorities, and the employees who received the options are in an uproar about possible tax consequences.

A suit is filed to set aside the option grants. Suppose the court sets them aside as *ultra vires* for having been issued in violation of the stock option plan and orders disgorgement of any gains on exercised options. Put aside the question of whether the recipient employees would have a contract claim for damages. Assume as a business matter that the corporation has to make the recipients whole by compensating them for the loss of the options and profits, and any adverse tax consequences. After all, they are valuable employees who,

---

[82] *See, e.g.,* Stephen M. Bainbridge, *Ryan v. Gifford: Chandler Tackles Stock Options,* at ProfessorBainbridge.com, http:// www.professorbainbridge.com/2007/02/ryan-v-gifford.html (Feb. 7, 2007).

[83] *E.g., id.* (arguing that if the backdated option grants are declared invalid as being *ultra vires,* there is no further harm to the corporation to justify derivative litigation against the board); *see also* Larry E. Ribstein, *Bainbridge and Chandler on Backdating,* at http://busmovie.typepad.com/ideoblog/2007/02/bainbridge-and-.html (Feb. 8, 2007) (agreeing that backdated options can be set aside as *ultra vires* and noting that although a disclosure violation would still remain, fashioning a remedy for the disclosure violation would be problematic).

through no fault of their own, found themselves in the midst of a controversy they did not create. They will be disgruntled if their reasonable expectations are not met.

The suit also contains allegations of breach of fiduciary duty and a claim for damages against the directors. The plaintiffs seek a remedy on behalf of the corporation for the costs of satisfying its employees, for the regulatory penalties it was forced to pay, and for the other economic consequences of the backdating, including, let's say, $12.5 million to cover the costs of the internal investigation.

In that circumstance, the appropriate measuring stick for director responsibility is that of equity. Why? Contrast these possible scenarios in which the board's compensation committee approves the options in question. In the first, which I will call "Scenario I," the compensation committee, although not acting with reasonable diligence, approves the option grants without realizing that the grants violate the terms of the stock option plan and without realizing that the corporation is accounting for them improperly. In fact, they are advised by the corporation's general counsel, HR director, and CFO that the grants were appropriate under the plan. The committee knew who was getting them, the incentives for performance they were intended to create, and the economic terms of the options, but it did not dig into the details, such as the actual date of the grants or the stock's trading price on those dates, after receiving reports from the key officers. Even assume that the committee signed a written consent or two, circulated to them by company counsel.

In the second situation, which I will call "Scenario II," assume by contrast that the compensation committee approved options grants to newly-hired employees, but was aware that the stockholder-approved option plan required options to be issued at fair market value on the date of grant. The committee realized that this was problematic because depending on market fluctuations in the stock price, employees hired in the same quarter could end up with very different incentives. Being told that "everyone was doing it," the committee decided to approve a plan of systematically backdating options so that recipients would all have a strike price set at the lowest price of the quarter in which they were hired. The committee was aware that the options were being accounted for as if they were issued on the date used to set the strike price when they in fact were not. By that means, there was no balance sheet impact to the corporation. Of course, this involved accounting fraud and tax fraud, but a little of that was perceived by the committee to be the emerging American way.

Without prejudging all the implications of these scenarios, it is fair to say that they present interesting questions about the culpability the compensation committee members have for harm caused to the corporation by the option grants. In Scenario I, there is a serious argument that the directors cannot be held liable in damages for breach of any duty. For starters, to find them liable for breach of fiduciary duty absent the exculpation clause, one would have to consider whether their failure to realize the impropriety of the options grants rose to a level of gross negligence, the higher threshold used by our law to analyze due care claims for several policy reasons that are well understood. But because they are protected by the exculpation clause, the directors can only be held liable if they act with a state of mind that is disloyal to their obligations to the corporation. In this context, that would likely require a finding that the compensation committee knew that the options violated the stock option plan and that the options were being accounted for in a manner that was improper, or that their failure to obtain that information resulted from their knowing abdication of their directorial duties. In other words, it is precisely by the careful use of equitable principles to analyze director conduct that directors are protected from liability in a situation when they did not act with scienter.

Likewise, in Scenario II, these principles reveal the directors' wide-open exposure to damages liability. Because the directors would have consciously taken action beyond their authority, they were, as explained in *Ryan* and *Tyson,* disloyal to the corporation. This is so even though their motives were not necessarily selfish. Although the directors may have had a reasonable business basis to provide the same incentives to all similarly situated employees, they did so using a technique (below-market options) that they had agreed not to use—and then lied about it. As the Chancellor explained in *Ryan* and *Tyson,* that deception is itself a disloyal act.[87]

By contrast, in a situation where directors are expressly permitted under the terms of a stockholder-approved option plan to issue below-market options, it would be well within the realm of business judgment to choose to issue all options to a set of similarly-situated employees at a uniform strike price reflecting the stock's low point for the quarter. But even in that situation, a director could not, with impunity, secretly backdate the option grants while falsely representing that they were made at fair market value on the dates of the grants or account for them as such. As illustrated by the financial restatements issued by Sycamore, options backdating has serious accounting implications and unless the options grants are properly accounted for—which would require taking a non-cash charge against earnings in the amount of the difference between the market price on the actual dates of the grants and the exercise price that reflects the earlier-lower trading prices, a consistent practice of options backdating can cause a company's financial statements to be materially misleading. This can expose the company to the regulatory consequences and civil and criminal liability that stem from knowingly issuing false earnings reports. Moreover, the tax implications of backdating cannot be ignored, and unless the company accounts for the backdated grants on its tax returns as below-market grants, it

---

[87] If the directors wanted to ensure that all employees hired around the same time have options with the same strike price, they could do so without violating the price restrictions of a stockholder-approved option plan by providing that all options awarded to employees hired in a particular quarter be granted at fair market value as of the first day of the quarter after the one in which the employees were hired. The same goal is achieved without the granting of below-market options.

could in some circumstances be found to have taken deductions to which it was not entitled. Alternatively, to the extent the recipients of the options do not recognize income to reflect the receipt of a below-market grant, they would be exposed to both additional taxes and penalties. In those situations, the company might be forced as either a legal or practical matter to make the affected employees whole, at the corporation's expense.

In short, by consciously causing the corporation to violate the law, a director would be disloyal to the corporation and could be forced to answer for the harm he has caused. Although directors have wide authority to take lawful action on behalf of the corporation, they have no authority knowingly to cause the corporation to become a rogue, exposing the corporation to penalties from criminal and civil regulators. Delaware corporate law has long been clear on this rather obvious notion; namely, that it is utterly inconsistent with one's duty of fidelity to the corporation to consciously cause the corporation to act unlawfully. The knowing use of illegal means to pursue profit for the corporation is director misconduct.

In this same vein, the importance and utility of the Delaware Supreme Court's recent decision in *Stone v. Ritter,*[90] reinforcing the vitality of this court's decision in *In re Caremark Int'l Inc. Deriv. Litig.,*[91] should not be ignored. Some respected scholars seem to fear that *Stone* opens directors to new kinds of claims foreclosed by *Caremark,*[92] while others read it as taking away a non-scienter based claim *Caremark* supposedly seemed to suggest.[93] Neither position seems entirely consistent with the decision itself. *Stone* clarified one of the most difficult questions in corporate law—when directors with no motivation to injure the firm can be held responsible if the corporation incurs serious harm as a result of its failure to obey the law. What *Stone* makes clear is that *Caremark* and its progeny, such as *Guttman v. Huang,*[94] are still good law. For reasons *Caremark* well-explained, to hold directors liable for a failure in monitoring, the directors have to have acted with a state of mind consistent with a conscious decision to breach their duty of care. *Caremark* itself encouraged directors to act with

---

[90] 911 A.2d 362 (Del.2006).

[91] 698 A.2d 959 (Del. Ch.1996).

[92] *E.g.,* Stephen M. Bainbridge, *Stone v. Ritter: Directors' Caremark Oversight Duties,* at ProfessorBainbridge.com, http:// www.professorbainbridge.com/2007/01/stone-v-ritter.html (Jan. 3, 2007) (suggesting that under *Stone,* a conscious decision by the board of directors that the costs of a formal law compliance program outweigh the benefits might result in *per se* liability).

[93] *E.g.,* Eric A. Chiappinelli, Delaware Supreme Court on Good Faith (Again) and the Duties of Care and Loyalty, at http:// businessentitiesonline.typepad.com/new-developments/2006/11/ delaware-suprem.html (Nov. 8, 2006) (suggesting that *Stone* had undercut *Caremark*'s recognition of an enforceable duty of care in the monitoring context).

[94] 823 A.2d 492 (Del. Ch.2003).

reasonable diligence, but plainly held that director liability for failure to monitor required a finding that the directors acted with the state of mind traditionally used to define the mindset of a disloyal director–bad faith–because their indolence was so persistent that it could not be ascribed to anything other than a knowing decision not to even try to make sure the corporation's officers had developed and were implementing a prudent approach to ensuring law compliance.[95] By reinforcing that a scienter-based standard applies to claims in the delicate monitoring context, *Stone* ensured that the protections that exculpatory charter provisions afford to independent directors against damage claims would not be eroded. *Stone* has obvious implications for cases like this, when a plaintiff seeks to hold directors accountable for failing to prevent backdating by corporate officers.

Even more than backdating, spring loading presents doctrinally-complex issues. Consider this example. A corporation has been engaged in serious efforts to land a so-called merger of equals. The CFO and COO have missed their summer vacations, their children's baseball games, and every important family occasion for four months, while working on the transaction. The CEO recommends to the independent compensation committee, whose members are protected by a § 102(b)(7) provision, that they make special awards of options as bonuses to the CFO and COO for their extraordinary efforts. The committee agrees that is warranted and makes the awards in advance of the announcement of the merger agreement, recognizing that the announcement will likely increase the company's stock price, as the company is the selling firm under the merger agreement. The corporation's stock option plan does not require that all options be issued at fair market value on the date of grant. In the merger proxy, it is clearly disclosed that the CFO and COO received the grants in recognition of their efforts in connection with securing the merger, that the options will vest and be exercisable if the merger is consummated, and that the corporation has accounted for the options as fair-market-value awards, in good faith reliance upon the advice of tax and accounting advisors that such treatment was literally consistent with applicable regulatory law, especially given that the merger was subject to several closing conditions. In this context, there would be no deception on the corporation's stockholders, as the directors would have fully disclosed why they made the award, and the compensation committee would seemingly be entitled to strong protection from both the § 102(b)(7) clause and § 141(e) of the Delaware General Corporation Law. All of these factors–the candor of the directors about

---

[95] *Caremark*, 698 A.2d at 968-70. In this respect, I do not read *Stone* as undercutting the discretion given to corporations to address law compliance in a manner that takes into account the precise circumstances facing the corporation. Rather, I read it as reaffirming the protection given by *Caremark* to directors who make good faith judgments about how their corporations should address law compliance, approaches that will obviously vary because of the different circumstances corporations confront.

the reason for the grant, their compliance with the terms of the relevant plan, and their good faith reliance on experts–would be of great relevance to a court considering whether a challenge to the grants stated a claim under *Tyson,* because they present a more traditional context in which the fundamental issue is whether the directors have made a rational compensation decision.

Indeed, one can make these facts even closer to *Tyson,* and still see complicating distinctions. Assume that all the facts are the same, except that the stock option plan approved by the stockholders expressly required grants to be made at fair market value. But further assume that the stockholders were told that the reason for that condition was singular and predicated solely on the desirability of having all grants qualify for favorable tax and accounting treatment. In fact, the disclosures to the stockholders in advance of the approval vote made clear that the stock option plan was, subject to such qualification, intended to permit the corporation to reward outstanding performance *and* to create incentives for superior future efforts. Under the carefully-crafted test articulated by the Chancellor in *Tyson,* these facts would arguably not give rise to anything other than an excess compensation claim, as it would be difficult to find that the defendants acted in a deceptive manner intended to circumvent the purposes of a stockholder-approved stock option plan.[98]

---

[98] As compared to backdated options–which inherently involve plain lies about the option grant date–so-called spring-loaded options do not clearly violate the literal terms of a fair-market-value restriction because such options are issued at the fair market value prevailing in public markets on the date of issuance. The factor driving the *Tyson* holding seemed to be that the fair-market-value restriction within that plan had been sold to stockholders as providing only incentives for future performance, not as a way to reward past performance, and that the spring-loaded issuances essentially breached an implied term of the plan. If, by contrast, a plan was sold to stockholders on the basis that use of a fair-market-value standard was advisable solely to ensure favorable tax and accounting treatment, the analysis would arguably be different. In that situation, the issue would be whether the company's possession of potentially market-moving non-public information would disqualify those options for the favorable tax and accounting treatment typically available for options granted at fair market value, and whether the board knew that to be so. Advice from professional advisors that they believed spring-loaded grants to be eligible for such treatment would be relevant in assessing the liability of directors. *See* [DGCL] § 141(e) ("A member of the board of directors ... shall ... be fully protected in relying in good faith upon ... any ... person as to matters the member reasonably believes are within [the] person's professional or expert competence."). Of course, there would remain the issue of deception. But if directors consciously granted options in advance of the issuance of positive information as a bonus, disclosed their motivations candidly, and accounted for the options in good faith reliance on experts, it is difficult to perceive the existence of a fiduciary duty claim other than for excess compensation. Because the directors would have disclosed their motivations openly, the state law obligations of fair disclosure would have been met. And because the parties to the option grant–the corporation and the recipients–were both aware of the information, it would be difficult to frame the transaction as insider trading under any prevailing theory.

By contrast, one could imagine how a lack of candor by the directors about the motivation for their actions could generate litigable issues. If directors were to engage in a pattern of awarding officers and themselves options in advance of announcements of positive news, setting the terms of

These examples, which present only a few of the many plausible scenarios in which interesting questions about stock option grants could arise, highlight the need for judicial caution. Lumping context-specific behavior involving varying motivations into generic categories such as backdating, spring loading, and bullet dodging, and driving results by such labeling, seems unlikely to do justice. I endeavor to keep that in mind as I address the implications of the three different categories of Grants that Desimone challenges. I begin with his attack on the Employee Grants.

D. *Desimone's Allegations About the Employee Grants Fail to Plead Demand Excusal*

The Employee Grants involve options grants of the type described in the Internal Memo, in which stock options issued to rank-and-file employees were deliberately backdated to reflect a strike price equal to the lowest trading price of the quarter, while at the same time represented to be, and accounted for as, fair-market-value grants. Reliance on the Internal Memo has allowed Desimone to make some detailed allegations about the way in which a conspiracy to backdate the Employee Grants was carried out. The financial restatement issued by Sycamore in 2005 admits that a number of Employee Grants made from 1999 to 2001 were improperly accounted for because the options were recorded as having been issued at fair market value, when they were in fact "in the money" as of the actual grant date and deceptively backdated to conceal that reality.

Plaintiff Desimone does not contend that any of Sycamore's directors are interested in the Employee Grants, or that they are incapable of acting independently of the recipients of the Grants. Therefore, the demand excusal analysis regarding these allegations focuses on whether any of the directors faces a substantial threat of personal liability. In that regard, although the fact that wrongdoing occurred is most obvious with respect to the Employee Grants, demand is also most clearly not excused with respect to this category. The Employee Grants were awarded pursuant to the Incentive Plan, which expressly contemplated both that Sycamore's board might delegate most of the option-granting functions to non-director executive officers and that the board itself might play a very minimal role in the option granting process. The complaint pleads no facts to suggest that any member of the board was involved in the

---

those awards to allow the recipients immediate rewards, and thereafter failing to be honest that that was what they were doing, the lack of disclosure might be relevant in determining whether the awards were motivated by the best interests of the corporation or an intent to stock the larders of those who toil on the top floor of the corporation's headquarters. Again, however, assuming proper tax and accounting treatment, the ultimate issue would turn on whether a proper compensation decision was made, rather than simply on the fact that the options were consciously granted in advance of the release of positive information.

details of the Employee Grants in any way, much less that the board was driving the process by, and dates on, which options were awarded.

Plaintiff Desimone next contends that even if the directors were ignorant of the backdating activity, that ignorance resulted from an abdication of the board's duty to monitor the corporation's compliance with applicable laws and regulations. He contends that Sycamore's internal controls were "woefully deficient," as evidenced by the ease with which the backdating operation was carried on and that, as a result, all of the Director Defendants, and particularly the three Audit Committee members, face a substantial likelihood of personal liability for "failing to adequately monitor Sycamore's financial reporting and to detect, prevent, and/or halt the modification of stock option grant dates and the material misstatements complained of herein."

In *Caremark,* Chancellor Allen explained that this type of lack of oversight claim "is possibly the most difficult theory in corporation law upon which a plaintiff might hope to win a judgment."[107] That statement has been quoted in a number of this court's decisions, and the Delaware Supreme Court recently reiterated this point in *Stone v. Ritter* by clarifying that this type of liability is founded upon a breach of the duty of loyalty. As *Guttman* stated and *Stone* reinforced, "imposition of liability [on this theory] requires a showing that the directors knew that they were not discharging their fiduciary duties."[108] "Only a sustained or systematic failure of oversight ... will establish the lack of good faith that is a necessary condition to liability."[109] Thus, in order to state a viable *Caremark* claim, and to predicate a substantial likelihood of director liability on it, a plaintiff must plead the existence of facts suggesting that the board knew that internal controls were inadequate, that the inadequacies could leave room for illegal or materially harmful behavior, and that the board chose to do nothing about the control deficiencies that it knew existed.[110]

Here, Desimone has not alleged any facts to suggest that Sycamore's internal controls were deficient, much less that the board, the Audit Committee, or Sycamore's auditors had any reason to suspect that they were or that backdating was occurring. Delaware courts routinely reject the conclusory allegation that because illegal behavior occurred, internal controls must have been deficient, and the board must have known so.

---

[107] 698 A.2d at 967.

[108] *Stone,* 911 A.2d at 370 (citing *Guttman,* 823 A.2d at 506).

[109] *Caremark,* 698 A.2d at 971.

[110] *Stone,* 911 A.2d at 373.

E. *Desimone Fails to Plead Demand Excusal
with Respect to the Officer Grants*

As with the Employee Grants, Desimone does not contend that any member of Sycamore's board is interested in the Officer Grants or dependent upon any Officer Grant recipient. Desimone's allegations with regard to these Officer Grants involve accusations of backdating as well as both spring loading and bullet dodging. Because the issues raised by the different allegations are distinct, I address them separately.

1. *Allegations of Backdating*

The allegedly backdated Officer Grants that Desimone challenges consist of two isolated sets of options grants that occurred in April 2001 and April 2002. Desimone points out that the dates of these Officer Grants followed steep market declines and immediately preceded a sharp upswing. He contends that such fortuitous timing shows that those options must also have been granted later and backdated to the time when the price was at its low point. For purposes of the present analysis, I will assume that all of the Officer Grants were in fact backdated.

Of course, large options grants to executive officers present a scenario in which it is far less likely that responsibility for the grants was delegated by the board. Indeed, I assume that it would have been improper for the board to have delegated authority to Frances Jewels, a recipient of two large options awards, to issue options to herself. As a result, although not directly alleged, it is reasonable, at this stage, to infer that Sycamore's Compensation Committee retained direct authority over the Officer Grants.

That does not mean, however, that I can infer that the Compensation Committee knowingly approved backdated options and Desimone has admitted that he cannot in good faith allege that any director did. In other words, the plaintiff admits that he has no idea how, when, or by whom the Officer Grants were issued. As stated, I can infer that the Compensation Committee approved the amount and recipients of the Officer Grants. But I can infer nothing from the pled facts about whether and to what extent any director was involved in the mechanics by which the options were issued or the dates on which that administrative task was carried out.

As important, Sycamore's Compensation Committee consisted of only two out of six board members, not half of the board as in *Ryan*. Thus, even assuming that the complaint established a substantial likelihood of personal liability on the part of the two Compensation Committee members, dismissal would be required unless the complaint established, through well-pled, particularized factual allegations, that at least one other board member is substantially likely to be personally liable, which it does not.

2. *Allegations of Spring Loading and Bullet Dodging*

In the previous section, analyzing Desimone's backdating allegations with respect to the Officer Grants, I assumed that all of the Officer Grants were in fact backdated. As I noted, I am not convinced that such an inference can be properly drawn from the complaint. As an alternative contention to his backdating claim, Desimone raises an argument that even if the Officer Grants were not actually backdated, one of the Officer Grants was improper because Sycamore manipulated the release of material non-public information in order for the options recipients to get the benefit of an artificially-low exercise price. The allegation is that on April 5, 2001, Sycamore announced that revenue and earnings for the third quarter would be lower than previously projected primarily due to low customer orders. Within a day of that announcement, Sycamore's stock price dropped from $9.06 to $7.25. The 2001 Officer Grants were dated April 9, when the stock price was at $7.39. Sixteen days later, on April 25, Sycamore made a positive announcement regarding its market share in the "European Metro DWDM market." Over the next week, Sycamore's share price trended generally upward, closing at a high of $12.02 on May 2.

These allegations combine elements of both bullet dodging (i.e., issuing options on the heels of a release of negative information) and spring loading (issuing options just before a release of positive information). Through them, Desimone hopes to make out a claim of disloyalty under the theory articulated in *Tyson,* which is that directors breach their fiduciary duties if they approve spring-loaded or bullet-dodging options in a bad faith effort to circumvent stockholder-approved restrictions on the exercise price of options. There are several important differences, however, between this case and *Tyson,* the most important of which for purposes of this claim is that the Incentive Plan, under which the Officer Grants were made, did not impose any such option exercise price restrictions. Rather, below-market options were expressly permitted by the Incentive Plan. Therefore, there were no rigid exercise price restrictions to circumvent.

With regard to the bullet dodging allegations, I am skeptical that a bare allegation that a board of directors made a discretionary issuance of stock options at the market stock price after releasing negative information can ever be sufficient in itself to state a claim of director disloyalty, even when a stockholder-approved option plan requires fair-market-value grants. In this regard, there is a material difference between spring loading and bullet dodging. With spring loading, a director is granting options at a time when he knows the company's stock is worth more than its market trading price because the market is ignorant of information that will affect the price. That is not so with bullet dodging. When a director grants options after a release of negative information, he does so at a time when the market has absorbed all existing information about the company.

I turn now to the allegation that the 2001 Officer Grants involved tainted spring loading because Sycamore released positive information sixteen days after those Grants. The exotic options practices of American corporations will undoubtedly generate multiple occasions for this court to ponder the complexities of spring-loaded options. To resolve the present case, I need not delve further into them because Desimone's complaint fails to plead particularized facts suggesting that Sycamore's directors knowingly spring loaded any options grants. As a result, even under the generous assumption that such an allegation without more would state a claim, demand is not excused.

Desimone's complaint simply does not allege that any director was aware of the positive information at the time the 2001 Officer Grants were made. Nor would it be reasonable to draw such an inference from the facts that are pled, given that the positive information was not released until more than two weeks after the Grants. This is crucial because in light of Sycamore's exculpatory charter provision, a scienter-based standard for liability applies in determining whether any director faces a threat of personal liability for these Grants.

Finally, because Sycamore's two Inside Directors, board Chairman Deshpande and President and CEO Smith, owned, between them, nearly a third of the company and did not receive any allegedly improper options grants, it is difficult to infer any motive on their part to enrich Sycamore's executive officers at the expense of its stockholders. Any undue enrichment of such officers would have come largely at Deshpande and Smith's own expense. Deshpande and Smith receive very little in the way of compensation for their services on behalf of the company and therefore the only way for them to benefit from their efforts as officers and directors is to increase shareholder value. As a result, Deshpande and Smith would seem to have been highly motivated only to grant options to executive officers on terms that provided the recipients with a strong incentive to perform well.

In sum, ... the complaint here contains weak allegations about a single alleged instance of spring loading involving information that did not even clearly affect the corporation's stock trading price, without identifying who was responsible for the spring loading or identifying any plausible motive on the part of an entirely disinterested board to improperly enrich the Officer Grant recipients. As a result, Desimone has failed to plead facts showing that Sycamore's directors face a substantial threat of liability with respect to his allegation that the 2001 Officer Grants were tainted by spring loading.

F. *The Allegations About the Outside Director Grants Fail to State a Claim*

I now turn to the allegations about the Outside Director Grants, which focus on two sets of options grants made pursuant to the Outside Director Plan to the four Outside Directors. As stated, the Outside Director Plan provided for an automatic grant of 30,000 market-price options to each Outside Director each year, effective as of the date of Sycamore's annual meeting. The challenged Outside Director Grants occurred on December 13, 2001 and December 18, 2003, respectively.

The allegation regarding the Outside Director Grants is essentially that they, like the Officer and Employee Grants discussed earlier, were very favorably timed, too much so to be a matter of luck, and therefore some misconduct must have occurred. The 2001 Grants were made with an exercise price of $4.60 per share. Ten days earlier, Sycamore's shares were trading at $5.14 apiece. Twenty days after the Grants, they were back up to $5.17. The 2003 Grants were made at an exercise price of $4.59 per share. Ten days earlier, Sycamore's shares traded at $4.94 apiece. Twenty days after the Grants, they were above $6. The complaint further points out that the 2001 and 2003 Outside Director Grants came shortly after (by about a month) the release of Sycamore's first quarter performance results in each of those two years, which occurred in the second week of November. Desimone contends that those disclosures contained negative information that caused Sycamore's stock price to trade downward in the following weeks so that when the options were granted pursuant to the Outside Director Plan in mid-December, the Outside Directors got the benefit of a lower exercise price than they otherwise would have had. In 2001, the first quarter results showed a decrease in revenue and a net loss of $247.9 million, which included a non-cash charge of $202.5 million. In 2003, the first quarter results reported a $12.2 million net loss.

Analysis of the Outside Director Grant allegations requires a different approach than that engaged in with respect to the Employee and Officer Grants. A majority of Sycamore's directors are recipients of the challenged Outside Director Grants. Demand is excused under the *Rales* test if a majority of the board is interested in the transaction being challenged. Because the Outside Directors received the Outside Director Grants and stand on the other side of the transaction from the company, they are interested in the sense that they have a personal financial stake in the challenged Grants that is at odds with the interests of Sycamore.

Moreover, when some of the directors are interested, the court must inquire whether any of the other directors are compromised in their ability to act independently of the directors found to be interested. In this regard, it is difficult to conclude that the two Inside Directors, Smith and Deshpande, can be deemed, for demand excusal purposes, independent of the Outside Directors. Although Smith and Deshpande are, to say the least, hardly among the most highly-compensated corporate executives in America, they nonetheless have a strong interest in remaining in their corporate offices. Those offices allow them, at the least, to exercise a large amount of personal control over their substantial–but not majority–equity investment in the company. Smith and Deshpande serve in their corporate offices by the grace of Sycamore's board, the majority of which is comprised of the very Outside Directors who would be defendants in any suit challenging the Outside Director Grants.

Therefore, because of the Outside Directors' interest in the challenged transactions, and the likely inability of the Inside Directors to act independently of them, the *Rales* test indicates that demand is excused with regard to the Outside Director Grants. I will assume for purposes of this analysis that demand is in fact excused on this basis. The inquiry in determining whether to allow the plaintiff to proceed past the pleading stage is therefore whether the complaint's allegations state a claim under the more lenient Rule 12(b)(6) standard.

The plaintiff initially contends that the beneficial timing of the 2001 and 2003 Outside Director Grants gives rise to an inference that those Grants were deliberately backdated and that the allegations state a claim under this court's holding in *Ryan*. That contention, however, is unsupported by pled facts. The Outside Director Grants occurred automatically each year on the date of Sycamore's annual stockholders meeting, which was scheduled far in advance. The complaint makes no allegation that the Grants were not in fact made on those pre-scheduled dates, nor does it allege that the dates of the meetings themselves were in any way manipulated to achieve a more beneficial option exercise price. In other words, the backdating allegation is contradicted by complaint itself and the documents it incorporates.

Desimone's marginally more colorable claim with respect to the Outside Director Grants is a bullet dodging allegation similar to the one he makes with respect to the 2001 Director Grants. The contention is that the challenged Grants came on the heels of a negative quarterly earnings report, which caused the stock price to go down and gave the Outside Directors the benefit of a lower exercise price for their options. As discussed, I am skeptical that bare allegations of this type in connection with an option plan that allows for discretionary options grants have any claim-sustaining relevance in light of the fact that the exercise price of the options is equal to a market price on the date of the grant that incorporates all existing material information. Even when an option plan requires fair-market-value grants, such grants fully comply with that restriction.

Therefore, if allegations that a company disclosed material information affecting its stock price in proximity to an automatic, regularly-scheduled option grant are to support a breach of fiduciary duty claim based on the theory accepted in *Tyson*, they must involve allegations that the company deviated from a regular disclosure pattern in a deceptive, non-candid effort to influence the exercise price of options and circumvent the intended functioning of the stockholder-approved option plan. But when, as here, the complaint simply alleges that the directors took the good and the bad that came with a non-discretionary plan, by receiving their options annually on the specified date regardless of the positive or negative nature of the regularly-issued quarterly report preceding the grants, no breach of fiduciary duty claim is stated.

For all of those reasons, the plaintiff's allegations regarding the Outside Director Grants fail to state a claim.

VII. *Conclusion*

For the reasons stated, the complaint is dismissed because plaintiff Desimone: (1) lacks standing to challenge options grants made before February 4, 2002, the date on which he first bought Sycamore shares; (2) has failed to plead demand excusal as to the allegations challenging the Officer and Employee Grants; and (3) has failed to state a claim upon which relief can be granted as to the allegations challenging the Outside Director Grants. Because these rulings also dispose of the claims against the Officer Defendants, I do not address their distinct arguments for dismissal. IT IS SO ORDERED.

Notes and Questions

1. Notes

a. The larger, corporate governance implications of the options backdating scandal are discussed in Chapter 14 below.

2. Reality Check

a. What is options backdating?

b. What are spring-loaded options?

c. What are bullet-dodging options?

d. Does Vice Chancellor Strine treat backdating, spring-loading, and bullet-dodging options in the same fashion?

e. What were the two options plans that Sycamore had? How were they different?

f. What were the three grants under scrutiny in this case? Does Vice Chancellor Strine treat them identically?

g. Did Sycamore engage in granting backdated, spring-loaded, or bullet-dodging options?

h. Why does Vice Chancellor Strine dismiss the complaint?

i. What was the plaintiff's theory of the case? Why did the Vice Chancellor not agree?

3. What Do You Think?

a. Do you think that backdating, spring-loading, and bullet-dodging options present the same dangers? What are they?

b. Are these option practices designed to hurt the corporation? If so, how? If not, how can a director or officer who approves such practices violate the duty of loyalty?

Pages 400-402
Delete the section titled "**B. BACKGROUND AND CONTEXT**"

Chapter 12
The Duty of Care of Directors (and Officers)

Page 410

Delete *In re Caremark International Inc. Derivative Litigation* and the associated Notes and Questions.

Chapter 13
Standards of Review of Board Actions

Page 437

Add the following before "**B. THE DUTY OF CARE**":

2. The *Caremark* Standard

ATR-Kim Eng Financial Corp. v. Araneta
2006 WL 3783520 (Del. Ch. Dec. 21, 2006)

STRINE, V.C.

I. *Introduction*

Plaintiffs ATR-Kim Eng Financial Corp. ("ATR Financial") and ATR-Kim Eng Capital Partners, Inc. ("ATR Capital") (collectively, "ATR") own 10% of the shares of a holding company–PMHI Holdings Corp. (f/k/a LBC Global Corp.) (the "Delaware Holding Company"). ATR claims that defendant Carlos Araneta, who controlled the remaining 90% of the Delaware Holding Company's equity and served as chairman of its board, caused the corporation to transfer its key assets–its ownership of several businesses worth over $35 million (the "LBC Operating Companies")–to members of his family in violation of his fiduciary duties. The Delaware Holding Company was formed precisely to enable ATR to share with Araneta in the benefits of owning the LBC Operating Companies. But, after Araneta denuded the Delaware Holding Company of those assets, ATR was left with only a minority stock ownership position in a floundering joint venture that it had undertaken with Araneta, a position that is worth very little. Meanwhile, Araneta and his family were left with sole control of the LBC Operating Companies, which, from the record, appear to be thriving.

    Furthermore, ATR claims that the other members of the board of directors of the Delaware Holding Company, defendants Hugo Bonilla and Liza Berenguer, are jointly and severally liable for this harm because they failed to take any steps to monitor Araneta and prevent his self-dealing. Bonilla was the head of Araneta's operations in the United States, and Berenguer served as the Chief Financial Officer of his worldwide enterprise. They essentially admit that they regarded themselves as mere employees of Araneta and failed to take any steps to fulfill their fiduciary duties to the Delaware Holding Company. As directors, they were charged with protecting the interests of their corporation and its stockholders. Yet, Bonilla and Berenguer allowed Araneta to do whatever he wanted, without any examination of whether his conduct benefited the Delaware Holding Company and all of its stockholders, rather than simply Araneta personally.

In this post-trial opinion, I find that Araneta breached his duty of loyalty by impoverishing the Delaware Holding Company for his own personal enrichment. Bonilla and Berenguer also breached their duty of loyalty. Having assumed the important fiduciary duties that come with a directorship in a Delaware corporation, Bonilla and Berenguer acted as—no other word captures it so accurately—stooges for Araneta, seeking to please him and only him, and having no regard for their obligations to act loyally towards the corporation and all of its stockholders. Such behavior is not indicative of a good faith error in judgment; it reflects a conscious decision to approach one's role in a faithless manner by acting as a tool of a particular stockholder rather than an independent and impartial fiduciary honestly seeking to make decisions for the best interests of the corporation. Although it is clearly the case that Araneta is the most culpable of the defendants, Bonilla and Berenguer are accountable for their complicity in his wrongful endeavors.

Bonilla and Berenguer will be held jointly and severally liable for the monetary judgment ....

II. *Factual Background*

These are the facts as I find them after trial.

A. *Overview of the Key Arrangements Between Araneta and ATR*

Before describing the origins of the current dispute between ATR and Araneta in more detail, it is useful to provide a basic overview of the parties and how they came to form the Delaware Holding Company.

Araneta first met ATR's chairman Ramon Arnaiz when they were in kindergarten in the Philippines. During their school days, Araneta and Arnaiz became close friends. After many years of friendship, the two fell out of touch as each embarked on his own career.

Araneta left the Philippines to attend college in the United States. After completing his studies, Araneta returned home to work in his family's business— an empire of companies run from the Philippines that share the initials LBC in their names (collectively, "LBC").[2] Araneta gained prominence by developing

---

[2] LBC Development Corp., a corporation organized and existing under the laws of the Philippines, was the primary holding company for the Araneta family businesses before the events giving rise to this dispute. Through this entity, the Aranetas owned the non-U.S. LBC Operating Companies that

LBC Express, Inc. (f/k/a LBC Air Cargo), a Philippine version of Federal Express, into an international money remittance business that facilitates and profits from wire transfers made by Filipino expatriates who have gone abroad to make a living but continue to support their families still living in the Philippines. As a result of his efforts, Araneta came to dominate and control LBC and is the ultimate manager for the thousands of employees working for LBC and the hundreds of locations owned by LBC around the globe.

Meanwhile, Arnaiz went into the financial services field. He gained prominence by spearheading the revitalization of a major financial firm's Hong Kong office. Following that success, Arnaiz ("A"), along with Manuel Tordesillas ("T") and Lorenzo Roxas ("R"), founded ATR, a Philippine corporation licensed to provide investment and financial services. From its creation, ATR has been essentially a capital provider, helping businesses raise capital and investing its own funds (and those of its investors) in various enterprises.

In the late 1990s, Araneta and Arnaiz reunited. At that time, Araneta turned to Arnaiz and ATR for investment banking assistance on behalf of his LBC enterprise. Initially, Araneta engaged ATR to search for capital and to prepare LBC for a public offering. After a while, however, the relationship changed.

In 1999, ATR began investigating an opportunity to purchase a controlling interest in The Professional Group Plans, Inc., a corporation that sold "pre-need" insurance policies designed to cover expenses (such as educational and health costs) that buyers expected to face in the future (the "Pre-Need Company"). Seeing potential synergies in this industry between ATR's financial acumen and LBC's logistical network, which was well-positioned to attract Filipino customers who had traditionally purchased these policies, Arnaiz offered to structure the investment in the Pre-Need Company as a joint enterprise with Araneta. After some negotiation, Araneta agreed to participate in the deal ATR proposed.

Based on this understanding, ATR and Araneta executed two contracts—an "Undertaking Agreement" and a "Joint Venture Agreement"—that set out the terms of their relationship and laid the groundwork for the Delaware Holding Company's incorporation. Through the Joint Venture Agreement, ATR and Araneta bought a controlling interest in the Pre-Need Company, and as part of this transaction, ATR advanced $3.922 million on Araneta's behalf (the "Advances"). In exchange for the Advances, Araneta pledged, in the Undertaking Agreement, to contribute the LBC Operating Companies along

---

provided courier and money remittance services in the Philippines and to Filipino expatriates working in other nations. The Aranetas also own LBC Holdings USA Corp. (overseen by defendant Bonilla), which serves Filipinos working in the United States.

with his newly acquired interest in the Pre-Need Company to a new holding company and to issue to ATR a 10% minority interest in that entity.

Likewise, to safeguard their joint investment in the Pre-Need Company, ATR and Araneta executed a Stockholders Agreement which they attached to their Joint Venture Agreement (the "Stockholders Agreement"). The Stockholders Agreement evenly divided the eight (out of ten) board seats secured by ATR's and Araneta's joint 80% interest in the Pre-Need Company, and unanimously appointed Topax Colayco, the residual 20% shareholder in the Pre-Need Company, to be its President and CEO.

Although the Undertaking Agreement did not require that the holding company it contemplated be a Delaware, or even an American, entity, Araneta perceived the United States as a favorable jurisdiction in which to raise capital and viewed Delaware as a tax haven. In particular, Araneta viewed a Delaware entity as a vehicle that could be used to access the American capital markets through an initial public offering of stock. As a result, in January 2000, Araneta incorporated the Delaware Holding Company and presented ATR with 3,000 of its shares (10%) while personally retaining control over the residual 27,000 shares (90%). Likewise, Araneta appointed and dominated the Delaware Holding Company's board of directors, which consisted of himself, defendant Berenguer (Araneta's niece and the CFO of the LBC group of companies), and defendant Bonilla (the head of LBC's U.S. operations).

B. *The Personal Nature of This Dispute*

ATR's claims against Araneta boil down to an allegation that he abused his position of control over the Delaware Holding Company. Specifically, ATR claims that Araneta transferred the LBC Operating Companies from the Delaware Holding Company to his children for no consideration without notice to ATR and without following the process required by Delaware law.

Araneta does not dispute that the LBC Operating Companies are now owned by his family or that ATR has no interest in those assets through its minority ownership of the Delaware Holding Company. He merely claims never to have transferred ownership of the LBC Operating Companies to the Delaware Holding Company in the first place. He says that ATR knew that. What he never says is why ATR would have made a nearly $4 million payment to acquire 10% of an entity with no valuable assets. Further, in the event that I conclude that he is lying when he says that the Delaware Holding Company never owned the LBC Operating Companies, Araneta offers only the half-hearted and wholly-illogical defense that he was permitted to reclaim the LBC Operating Companies without payment through an accounting "offset" because he was the one who initially contributed the LBC Operating Companies to the Delaware Holding Company.

To understand how a case as stark as this actually resulted in a trial, rather than a voluntary settlement by Araneta, it is useful to return to Araneta's relationship with his old friend, Ramon Arnaiz. That's right, this case is personal.

But, as a result of their business dealings, Araneta's friendship with Arnaiz has ended. Araneta testified that he considers this case a "personal fight" between himself and Ramon Arnaiz. He stated in his deposition and confirmed at trial that he did not think his co-directors had "anything to do with this tie-up with ATR." And, perhaps most tellingly, he admitted on cross examination that at least "to some extent" this litigation was "over the disintegration of [his] friendship" with Arnaiz.

That disintegration began in November 2002 when ATR sold its 50% interest in Professional Holdings, the corporation that owned 80% of the Pre-Need Company. Having closely aligned himself with Arnaiz and ATR, Araneta felt betrayed by that action. In compliance with the Shareholders Agreement, which secured ATR's right to sell its Professional Holdings shares as long as Araneta was given a right of first refusal, ATR offered its shares to Araneta, but he refused to purchase them. After Araneta declined, ATR sold its interest to Topax Colayco (the "Colayco Sale") giving Colayco co-equal control with Araneta over Professional Holdings and thus over Professional Holdings's 80% control bloc in the Pre-Need Company. But, because Colayco already directly owned the residual 20% of the Pre-Need Company that Professional Holdings did not, Araneta understandably viewed himself as having less leverage than Colayco in this dynamic.

Notwithstanding ATR's contractual right to sell its interest in Professional Holdings and Araneta's own failure to exercise his right of first refusal, Araneta felt victimized by Arnaiz and ATR and blamed them for subjugating him to the role of a minority investor under Colayco's de facto control.

Araneta allowed this hostility to affect his management of the Delaware Holding Company. After the Colayco Sale, Araneta withheld information, effectively closed the lines of communication with ATR, and eventually transferred all of the LBC Operating Companies out of the Delaware Holding Company.

C. *The Discovery of Araneta's Misconduct*

Araneta began to exact his revenge soon after the Colayco Sale was completed. In the months that followed, ATR repeatedly requested information on the condition of the Delaware Holding Company in which it still had nearly $4 million invested. But Araneta summarily rebuffed those requests. Araneta testified that any request ATR made for information during the entire 2003 calendar year went ignored because he was "no longer talking to them because [he was] upset with Mr. Arnaiz."

Starved for information, ATR filed an action under [DGCL] § 220 in this court on October 27, 2003. But still irked by ATR's decision to sell its interest in Professional Holdings, Araneta "deliberately ignored" that lawsuit and instructed Bonilla not to provide the requested information.

Only after being ordered by this court to turn over the records requested by ATR did Araneta do so. On January 14, 2004, Araneta produced a "Compliance" that purported to include all available documents but totaled only nine pages and failed to include many essential corporate papers. The nine pages that Araneta did produce, however, included three documents that caused ATR great concern. Those documents–two balance sheets and a purported resolution of the board of directors–led ATR to believe that Araneta had conducted a de facto (and non-pro rata) liquidation of the Delaware Holding Company's assets and that Araneta was attempting to escape responsibility for that act.

These financial statements indicated that during the last nine months of 2003 Araneta stripped the Delaware Holding Company of the LBC Operating Companies. The only operating asset he left in the Delaware Holding Company was ownership of the de facto minority position in the Pre-Need Company.

D. *The Parties' Claims*

Based on the balance sheets unearthed in the § 220 action, ATR filed this lawsuit on June 3, 2004. ATR claims that it was harmed as a stockholder of the Delaware Holding Company when Araneta effectively made a $36 million liquidation payment to his family without following the required process and without distributing to ATR its pro rata portion thereof. ATR also alleges that the corporation itself was injured by this transaction because it received no substantial consideration for the transfer of substantially all of its assets to the Araneta family.

In response, Araneta mounted three shifting defenses. If his implausible excuses were not expending ATR's and this court's limited resources and impeding ATR's just claim for recompense, Araneta's brazen and abundant falsehoods might be amusing. Because they have these costs, they are appalling.

III. *Legal Analysis*

ATR's allegations against Araneta are clear-cut claims of self-dealing by a controlling shareholder and director of a Delaware corporation. [I] have found as a fact that Araneta removed from the Delaware Holding Company its primary assets–its ownership of the LBC Operating Companies. In its financial statements and tax filings, the Delaware Holding Company had valued this ownership interest at over $36 million. Yet, by the end of 2003, this value had disappeared from the Delaware Holding Company's books. To where did Araneta remove the assets? To his family. What did the Delaware Holding Company receive in exchange? Effectively nothing. Araneta did not even reduce his 90% interest in the Delaware Holding Company when he repossessed the very assets that had secured that interest in the first place. Araneta simply took the LBC Operating Companies back in a fit of pique.

The evidence in this case is clear, and Araneta's attempts to distort that reality only make his conduct less tolerable. Araneta used his majority control and effective dominion over the Delaware Holding Company and its board of directors to engage in a course of unfair dealing that resulted in a de facto liquidation of corporate assets that enriched the Araneta family at the expense of the Delaware Holding Company and ATR.

I now come to a slightly more difficult issue. Namely, to what extent should Araneta's fellow directors, Bonilla and Berenguer, share responsibility for harming the Delaware Holding Company and ATR?

Making this more challenging is that ATR does not allege that either Berenguer or Bonilla participated in, approved of, or directly profited from Araneta's removal of the LBC Operating Companies. Rather, ATR claims that Bonilla and Berenguer consciously breached the important duties articulated in this court's *Caremark* [112] decision and recently reaffirmed by our Supreme Court in *Stone v. Ritter*.[113] Specifically, ATR alleges that Bonilla and Berenguer failed to monitor Araneta's conduct thereby allowing his self-dealing to continue.

Under Delaware law, it is fundamental that a director cannot act loyally towards the corporation unless she tries–i.e., makes a genuine, good faith effort– to do her job as a director.[114] One cannot accept the important role of director in a Delaware corporation and thereafter consciously avoid any attempt to carry out one's duties.

One of the most important duties of a corporate director is to monitor the potential that others within the organization will violate their duties. Thus, "a director's obligation includes a duty to attempt in good faith to assure that a corporate information and reporting system, which the board considers to be adequate, exists."[115] Obviously, such a reporting system will not remove the possibility of illegal or improper acts, but it is the directors' charge to "exercise a good faith judgment that the corporation's information and reporting system is in concept and design adequate to assure the board that appropriate information

---

[112] *In re Caremark Int'l, Inc. Deriv. Litig.*, 698 A.2d 959 (Del. Ch.1996).

[113] 911 A.2d 362 (Del.2006).

[114] *See Guttman v. Huang,* 823 A.2d 492, 506 & n. 34 (Del. Ch.2003).

[115] *Caremark,* 698 A.2d at 970.

will come to its attention in a timely manner as a matter of ordinary questions, so that it may satisfy its responsibility."[116] Thus, as the Supreme Court recently stated:

> *Caremark* articulates the necessary conditions predicate for director oversight liability: (a) the directors utterly failed to implement any reporting or information system or controls; or (b) having implemented such a system or controls, consciously failed to monitor or oversee its operations thus disabling themselves from being informed of risks or problems requiring their attention. In either case, imposition of liability requires a showing that the directors knew that they were not discharging their fiduciary obligations. Where directors fail to act in the face of a known duty to act, thereby demonstrating a conscious disregard for their responsibilities, they breach their duty of loyalty by failing to discharge that fiduciary obligation in good faith.[117]

From the testimony of the directors of the Delaware Holding Company, it is apparent that no reporting system was in place and that no other information systems or controls were ever considered, let alone implemented, by the Delaware Holding Company's board of directors. They did not even have regular board meetings. As a result, the directors were often unaware of corporate activities–despite how easy that would have been given the Delaware Holding Company's modest size. Berenguer testified that although there had been meetings regarding the Delaware Holding Company before the LBC Operating Companies were transferred into the corporation in January 2001, she did not remember any meetings of the board of directors or of the shareholders after that time. Bonilla confirmed this fact, explaining that when the Delaware Holding Company's name was changed from LBC Global, Corp. to PMHI Holdings, Corp., he was never informed about the change, never voted to approve it, and did not even know what the initials PMHI in the new corporate name stood for at the time he signed the certificate of amendment as the corporation's authorized agent. Even when corporate activities involved them directly, ... neither Berenguer nor Bonilla questioned the wisdom of Araneta's actions nor insisted that corporate procedures be followed.

Moreover, both Berenguer and Bonilla testified that they entirely deferred to Araneta in matters relating to the Delaware Holding Company. Berenguer is, as mentioned, Araneta's niece and served as the CFO for the LBC group of companies worldwide. She testified that she would not insert herself into a disagreement between ATR and Araneta about how the Delaware Holding Company should proceed on an issue because such a disagreement would be

---

[116] *Id.*

[117] *Stone,* 911 A.2d 362.

between those parties and would not affect her as a director of the Delaware Holding Company. Similarly, she stated that she would take Araneta's word as authoritative if he claimed that he had agreed with ATR to take certain actions. Bonilla, the head of Araneta's U.S. operations, was more explicit—explaining that to him Araneta and the Delaware Holding Company were basically one and the same and that he took the word of Araneta as being the word of the company. Moreover, when pressed regarding whether he would undertake an independent inquiry if told to act by Araneta, Bonilla responded, "Why should I ask him all these questions? He's telling me they have already agreed .... It's not like I'm going to go out there and check on him, doesn't make sense."

Based on these failures, neither Berenguer nor Bonilla can be said to have upheld their fiduciary obligations. Although it was Araneta who ran amok by emptying the Delaware Holding Company of its major assets, the other directors did nothing to make themselves aware of this blatant misconduct or to stop it.

Put in plain terms, it is no safe harbor to claim that one was a paid stooge for a controlling stockholder. Berenguer and Bonilla voluntarily assumed the fiduciary roles of directors of the Delaware Holding Company. For them to say that they never bothered to check whether the Delaware Holding Company retained its primary assets and never took any steps to recover the LBC Operating Companies once they realized that those assets were gone is not a defense. To the contrary, it is a confession that they consciously abandoned any attempt to perform their duties independently and impartially, as they were required to do by law. Their behavior was not the product of a lapse in attention or judgment; it was the product of a willingness to serve the needs of their employer, Araneta, even when that meant intentionally abandoning the important obligations they had taken on to the Delaware Holding Company and its minority stockholder, ATR.

When required by their office to be loyal to the Delaware Holding Company, Bonilla and Berenguer chose total fealty to Araneta's conflicting interests instead. Consequently, I find them jointly liable for Araneta's fiduciary violations.

IV. *Conclusion*

Based on the foregoing, I find in favor of ATR on each of its claims and award ATR $3,922,000 in damages plus pre-judgment as well as post-judgment interest on this amount.

Notes and Questions

1. Notes

a. Vice Chancellor Strine imposed attorney fees on Mr. Araneta but not Mr. Bonilla or Ms. Berenguer.

2. Reality Check

a. What is the standard of review for *Caremark* claims?

b. How is the analysis different for Mr. Araneta, Mr. Bonilla, and Ms. Berenguer?

c. Vice Chancellor Strine wrote, "ATR does not allege that either Berenguer or Bonilla participated in, approved of, or directly profited from Araneta's removal of the LBC Operating Companies." Why, then, are Ms. Berenguer and Mr. Bonilla liable?

d. The court also held, "Under Delaware law, it is fundamental that a director cannot act loyally towards the corporation unless she tries–i.e., makes a genuine, good faith effort–to do her job as a director." Is this the statement of the duty imposed by *Caremark*?

e. Is there causation between the corporation's harm and Mr. Bonilla's and Ms. Berenguer's behavior?

3. What Do You Think?

a. Do you agree with the standard of review for *Caremark* claims? If not, what standard of review would you use?

b. Do you think successful *Caremark* claims will be frequent?

c. Is this really a *Caremark* claim against Mr. Bonilla and Ms. Berenguer? Isn't it just a duty of loyalty claim? If so, what is the consequence in terms of the standard of review?

d. Do you agree with Vice Chancellor Strine that it would have been "easy" for Mr. Bonilla and Ms. Berenguer to become aware of the corporation's activities? If not, why are they liable?

Page 489

Add the following before "**2. Suppose**":

The Delaware Supreme Court affirmed Chancellor Chandler's findings in June 2006.

Chapter 14
Do the Restrictions Work?

Page 536

Add the following before "**2. Systemic Problem or Cyclical Anomalies?**":

a. The Backdated Options Scandal

In 2006, the Wall Street Journal documented the fact that a large number of public corporations had engaged in backdating options. The Journal received the Pulitzer Prize for Public Service for that reportage. One consequence of that investigation was the *Desimone* case, above. The next readings describe and evaluate the backdating controversy. As you read the articles, ask yourself how backdating is similar to, and different from, the behavior that Enron and WorldCom engaged in. Also ask yourself whether the outside critics of corporate behavior were a cause of the controversy.

Mark Maremont and Charles Forelle, *Bosses' Pay: How Stock Options Became Part of the Problem*
Wall St. J. (Dec. 27, 2006)

Eugene Isenberg is the little-known chief executive of a modest-sized oil-services company in Houston. But he stands out in one way: He is among the highest-paid corporate executives in history. In the past 19 years, he has pocketed more than $450 million.

The key to this wealth: stock options, in abundance. His employer, Nabors Industries Ltd., has lavished more than 25 million options on him over the years.

They became lucrative partly because of Nabors's generally rising stock price, but also because of some controversial moves that gave the options more punch.

Stock options were hailed two decades ago as a remedy for runaway executive pay. Academics, politicians and investors, tired of seeing CEOs pocket big money for a so-so job, pushed to have stock options become a primary method of compensating executives. Options–granting the right to buy stock tomorrow at today's price–would pay off only if the company's stock went up. To advocates they were the ideal carrot, an incentive for good work that aligned executives' interests with those of shareholders.

That happened—sometimes. But at many companies, options morphed into the biggest executive bonanza yet, pouring out cash like a stuck ATM, and sorely disappointing those who thought options would moderate executive pay.

Instead of replacing big bonuses, options became an additional form of pay slathered on top of already-generous packages. Employers doled out options in ever-growing numbers, in part because, until recently, accounting rules meant companies didn't have to treat this largess to executives as an expense. And like Nabors, some used ... tactics that made it even easier for executives to score huge hauls.

This year, options practices exploded in one of the biggest corporate-fraud scandals in decades. Some companies and executives stole from shareholders, by pretending that options had been issued earlier than they really were, at more favorable prices. At least 130 U.S. corporations are under investigation for possible backdating of option grants. Some have admitted to it. More than 60 executives and directors of public companies have lost their jobs so far, 17 of them chief executive officers. After probable backdating was exposed at giant insurer UnitedHealth Group Inc., the CEO had to resign and give up about $200 million of stock-options value. The company said it will have to restate past earnings by as much as $1.7 billion.

Nabors's Mr. Isenberg offers an example of the huge wealth CEOs have gained through stock options. Now, some of his option grants appear to raise questions about how they were dated. A number came on days when the stock hit its lowest close for the month or the quarter. At other companies, a series of low-price grants has been a pattern that has suggested possible dating problems. At the least, the favorable grant dates added to Mr. Isenberg's mammoth options gains.

The backdating scandal at scores of companies shows one way stock options, once seen as an executive-pay reform, have often been distorted by corporate officials and their consultants. Nell Minow, a longtime corporate-governance advocate, calls backdating "just another in an endless and unstoppable series of mechanisms to subvert the purpose of stock options." A vocal proponent of options in the early 1990s, Ms. Minow now regrets that stance. "Options became completely disconnected from shareholder interests," she says. "I grossly underestimated the capacity of corporate boards and corporate managers to circumvent the principles we established."

Defenders of options, who remain numerous, say options shouldn't be judged by a few giant packages. Many companies have given out options judiciously, say defenders, some of whom attribute rising executive pay to tight competition for top managers. Others say stock options have helped to foster innovation, by giving young but cash-poor companies a currency with which to attract talent.

Some supporters of options even give them partial credit for the long bull market that began in 1982, figuring that options help focus top executives on the key issue for shareholders: the stock price. Frederic W. Cook, a New York compensation consultant, calls the stock option "the most perfect equity derivative that's ever been invented: It's simple, elegant, easily understood, and it gives you a little piece of the action."

Stock options usually give recipients a 10-year window to buy the company's stock at the price when the options are granted. If someone gets options when the stock trades at $50 and it goes to $75, the holder can cash out at the $50 "exercise price"–also called a "strike price"–and nail a $25 profit on each option. Options usually don't "vest," or become exercisable, for at least a year after they're granted.

Stock options appeared at least as early as the 1920s, says Carola Frydman, an assistant professor of finance at Massachusetts Institute of Technology who has studied the history of executive pay. The modern era began in 1950, when Congress, reversing a court ruling, gave options substantial tax advantages over ordinary income. By the middle of that decade, they accounted for nearly a third of CEO compensation at large industrial companies.

"In the 1950s, they called it the period of stock-option opulence," says Ms. Frydman. "They didn't know what was coming."

After losing popularity during the weak stock market of the 1970s, options surged back into favor in the late 1980s. One reason was public fury over mammoth executive paydays for bosses with just average performance. In an influential 1990 Harvard Business Review article, Mr. Murphy and Michael C. Jensen said the problem was executives were paid like "bureaucrats" instead of entrepreneurs. They called for giving "big rewards for superior performance and big penalties for poor performance."

"We were suggesting people shift from salaries to stock options to put more pay at risk," Mr. Murphy says today. But "that's not what companies ended up doing. They layered on massive amounts of options on top of the rest."

The bandwagon got two big boosts from an unlikely source: Congress.

First, it passed a law, pushed by President Clinton, seeking to rein in executive pay by limiting the tax break for it. The 1993 law said companies couldn't deduct yearly compensation of more than $1 million for any one of their top five officers.

But it exempted certain kinds of pay linked to performance, which included stock options. Companies rushed to restructure pay plans to grant more options. In 1994, the first year the law was in effect, the value of option grants to CEOs at S&P 500 firms leapt by 45% on average, according to Mr. Murphy, and nearly doubled again over the next two years.

The 1993 law "deserves pride of place in the Museum of Unintended Consequences," said Christopher Cox, chairman of the Securities and Exchange Commission, this fall.

Then in 1994, Congress helped beat back a proposed rule requiring companies to treat a stock-option grant as an expense and deduct it from profits. The plan, backed by the SEC and accounting rule makers, sparked intense corporate opposition. Congress stepped in to fight it, and after a long battle, the accounting rule makers caved. They issued a watered-down rule saying all that companies had to do was disclose in a footnote what options would have done to their profits, had the proposal passed.

Meanwhile, Congress left alone an older law that gave companies a tax deduction whenever stock options were exercised. Under that rule, which applied to the most common type of option given to executives, the employer can deduct a dollar from its income for tax purposes for every dollar of option gains pocketed by employees.

With rules like these, "what wasn't there to like about a stock option?" says Paula Todd, a compensation expert at consulting firm Towers Perrin. "You could grant them in unlimited amounts, with no expense, and claim a tax deduction. [Companies] would pay their dry cleaners if they could with stock options."

Soon, other forces spurred companies to give executives ever more stock options. One was the "Lake Wobegon effect," named for the mythical Minnesota town in radio host Garrison Keillor's world where all the children are above average. Many boards believed their chiefs should be paid at least as much as the average in their industry, and often more. That attitude had the effect of pushing this average up, year after year.

The options-issuing frenzy reached a peak in 1999 and 2000. Dot-com companies, some with little other way to pay employees, handed out options like confetti. Thousands of people made fortunes on stratospheric rises in the stocks of tech firms, some of which didn't exist a couple of years later. Meanwhile, some "old economy" companies, trying not to lose top people to Silicon Valley, cranked up their own options generators.

In mid-2002, Alan Greenspan testified to Congress about what was then a tech and telecom bust, and about a wave of corporate scandals at firms like Enron, WorldCom and Tyco International. The Federal Reserve's then-chairman spoke of an "infectious greed" that seemed to grip some in business, for which he partly blamed "poorly structured" stock options. Giant grants "perversely created incentives to artificially inflate reported earnings in order to keep stock prices high and rising," he said. "The incentives they created overcame the good judgment of too many corporate managers."

[R]ule changes have also helped slow the options express. Besides a 2002 requirement for prompt disclosure of grants, a new accounting rule means companies must record an expense when they make an options grant, and reduce profits accordingly. Many companies have cut back on options, and some have stopped awarding them at all, often replacing them with grants of shares.

Over the years, few corporate executives have availed themselves more thoroughly of what options have to offer than Nabors's Mr. Isenberg.

Still chief executive at the age of 77, Mr. Isenberg lives in the Breakers resort complex in Palm Beach, Fla., and commutes to Nabors's U.S. headquarters in Houston. A generous donor, he has helped found a school in New York for children with learning disabilities and given millions to the University of Massachusetts at Amherst, which has named its business school after him.

Mr. Isenberg worked at Exxon for 13 years and then headed a small steel company, settling into early retirement after that firm was sold in 1982. He was persuaded to rejoin the business world by his friend Martin Whitman, a prominent New York investor, whose fund had taken control of a troubled oil-services company called Anglo Energy. Mr. Isenberg invested some of his own money and in 1987 took the helm of what was soon renamed Nabors Industries.

The CEO's overall stock-option gains, both realized and not yet cashed in, came to $685 million at the end of last year, says S&P ExecuComp—putting him 8th on its list of big winners from 1992 to 2005.

Mr. Isenberg also has benefited from some good timing of his option grants. The Sept. 23, 1991, award was dated on the day Nabors's stock touched its lowest closing price of that month, $5.

But it isn't clear when the price was actually set. Company documents suggest the grant price may actually have been determined many months earlier, on another day when the stock closed at $5. Moreover, the grant was contingent on a new Isenberg employment contract—which other documents indicate wasn't signed until well after Sept. 23, when the stock was higher.

For a grant of a million options dated Dec. 4, 1995, another monthly low, Nabors produced no minutes of a compensation-committee meeting. Instead, a memo seven weeks later said there had been a discussion on Dec. 4 of Mr. Isenberg trading in part of his bonus for options. The memo said the idea first would be run by a consultant, suggesting the grant wasn't made final until weeks after the stated Dec. 4 award date.

In all, of 11 new option grants to Mr. Isenberg between 1991 and 2002, two were dated at quarterly lows in the Nabors stock price and five more at monthly lows. The odds against such a fortunate pattern occurring by chance are long.

In mid-2002, a federal law required executives to report option grants within two days after they're made, instead of having weeks or months to do so, a change that sharply cut the potential for backdating. Since mid-2002, none of Mr. Isenberg's four option grants came at monthly stock lows.

[Nabors' spokesperson Denny] Smith noted that before June 2002, Nabors was registered in Delaware, and directors could meet on short notice. Nabors then became a Bermuda-registered company. Mr. Smith said that since then it has had most board meetings outside the U.S., with options awarded at meetings "scheduled long in advance."

Mr. Isenberg has received compensation "beyond expectations," Mr. Smith said, because of Nabors's prosperity. The spokesman said Nabors is discussing a restructuring of Mr. Isenberg's future pay arrangement. Meanwhile, he has voluntarily cut the bonus he's entitled to in half.

Alan Murray, *Will Backdating Scandal Thwart Effort to Roll Back Reforms?*
Wall St. J. (Dec. 20, 2006)

A few bad apples. That was the oft-heard line taken by corporate leaders back in 2002 and 2003, after the meltdowns of Enron, WorldCom, Tyco and Parmalat. A few miscreants, they argued, shouldn't be allowed to tarnish the entire corporate world.

But this year's backdating scandal has eliminated the last echoes of that defense. More than 120 companies have been implicated in what all but a few hardy holdouts now acknowledge is simple theft. As one former chairman of the Business Roundtable told me: "Those guys were caught with their hands in the cookie jar."

Clearly, something's amiss in the orchard. A new study out this week helps explain what that might be. Three scholars–Lucian Bebchuk, Yaniv Grinstein, and Urs Peyer–have run the numbers on 29,000 grants of stock options to directors, and found that 9% of them were "lucky"–that is, they occurred on a day when the stock price hit a monthly low. "Lucky" is in quotes, because the authors clearly believe that many, if not most, were the result not of luck but of backdating.

One ... finding of note: The "lucky" grants were more common in the days before Sarbanes-Oxley, which sets tight deadlines for reporting option grants. But they continued after the corporate-reform law was passed, suggesting the problem hasn't been solved.

The backdating brouhaha has occurred just as the business community is gearing up to roll back rules put into place after the 2002-2003 scandals. The Securities and Exchange Commission last week announced plans to relax Sarbanes-Oxley requirements for smaller companies. In addition, the Justice Department said it was revising some of the tougher prosecution practices it adopted in the wake of those scandals. And the Committee on Capital Markets Regulation, a private group acting with the blessing of Treasury Secretary Hank Paulson, recently recommended more sweeping changes, including measures to limit class-action securities lawsuits.

The prevalence of backdating raises the question: Has the corporate-reform movement really gone too far? Or has it not gone far enough?

Assemble a room full of CEOs and you will find no doubt that it has gone too far. They'll regale you with stories about the excesses of litigation, the terror tactics of prosecutors who threaten to indict entire companies and the pointless costs of Sarbanes-Oxley Section 404, which requires outside audits of companies' internal financial controls. Fill the room with unionists, shareholder advocates and academics, and you'll hear tirades against the inconceivable greed of CEOs, who despite eight-figure paychecks feel the need to break the rules to make even more money.

In the midst of this rancorous debate, Ira Millstein, who has long labored in corporate governance, is the rare voice of sanity. Mr. Millstein, senior partner at Weil, Gotshal & Manges, rightly argues that some of the post-Enron reforms have gone too far. Indeed, he surprised and angered many of his left-leaning friends in academia and elsewhere by signing on to the report of the Committee on Capital Markets Regulation.

Many of those recommendations make good sense. Section 404 of Sarbanes Oxley was a classic case of legislative overreach, imposing excessive burdens on small companies, and discouraging foreign companies from listing shares in the U.S. The Justice Department's much-discussed "Thompson memo" was also the product of overreaction, allowing federal prosecutors to adopt the bullying tactics favored by New York's former attorney general, Eliot Spitzer. And class-action securities lawsuits, while not new, continue to be an overused tool. On all of these, some rollback would be welcome.

But in return for those changes, Mr. Millstein wants "the grand bargain." Instead of more regulation, more prosecution and more litigation, give shareholders more power to oversee the companies in which they invest. Make it clear, once and for all, that directors really do work for shareholders, not for management, by giving shareholders the power not only to remove directors, but also to nominate them, without engaging in costly proxy battles.

The commissioners of the SEC are considering changes that move in this direction, and the business lobby in Washington has launched a determined battle to stop them. For corporate leaders, shareholder democracy may be a frightening prospect. But it beats the alternatives.

Notes and Questions

1. Notes

a. You may wish to re-read *Desimone* in Chapter 11.

2. Reality Check

a. How is the backdating controversy similar to, and different from, Enron and WorldCom?

b. Is the backdating controversy of the same magnitude as Enron and WorldCom?

c. How were corporations that engaged in backdating harmed?

3. What Do You Think?

a. Isn't the backdating controversy just one of disclosure? If the corporations had made full disclosure of their actions, would any harm have resulted?

b. Isn't backdating simply a way of awarding recipients more compensation? If so, presumably the corporation could have given the recipient the additional compensation in cash. Given that, is backdating wrong?

c. Why did the post-Enron governance reforms not prevent backdating?

d. If backdating is a problem, what is the solution?

e. Are corporate governance reformers likely to succeed in their efforts? You may wish to re-read C.A. Harwell Wells' article on page 372 of the casebook about the cycles of corporate responsibility.

Chapter 15
Shareholder Governance Powers: Paradigms and Public Companies

Page 553
Add the following case before "**iii. Quorum**":

Accipiter Life Sciences Fund, L.P. v. Helfer
905 A.2d 115 (Del. Ch. 2006)

LAMB, Vice Chancellor.

A corporation announced its annual stockholder's meeting in a press release devoted mainly to financial results. A substantial stockholder failed to thoroughly read the document, failed to notice the stockholder meeting announcement, and thus failed to realize that, under the corporation's advance notice bylaw, it had ten days from the date of that public announcement to nominate a slate of directors to the board. It discovered its mistake two months later when its then belated attempts to nominate candidates were rebuffed for tardiness. It then sued to overturn the results of the uncontested election.

The stockholder concedes that two of its employees read the document on the day it was released, that those employees would have understood the disclosure to require haste had they read the crucial paragraph, and that it could have met the ten-day deadline. Nevertheless, it seeks equitable relief setting aside the election, claiming that the company's decision to place the announcement of the annual meeting in that particular press release constituted an inequitable manipulation of the corporation's election machinery. Largely because the important annual meeting announcement was readily and easily available, the court rejects that argument and grants summary judgment in favor of the defendants.

I.

A. *The Parties*

Accipiter is a self-described hedge fund based in New York which focuses its investments on companies in the healthcare sector. It consists of five full-time employees, including the General Partner, Gabe Hoffman, and Nicole Viglucci, the senior analyst responsible for covering LifePoint Hospitals, Inc. Accipiter, either directly or through affiliates, purports to own approximately 1.4% of LifePoint's shares.

LifePoint is a Delaware corporation engaged in providing healthcare services in rural communities. It was established on May 11, 1999, as a spin-off of HCA, Inc. The eight individual defendants comprise all of the members of LifePoint's board of directors. One of these directors, Kenneth C. Donahey, is a member of management. The remaining seven directors are independent of the corporation.

B. *The Facts*

1. *LifePoint's Advance Notice Bylaw*

LifePoint's bylaws require that the board of directors set the date of the corporation's annual stockholders meeting. In the past, the board has usually scheduled that meeting around the anniversary of LifePoint's creation. Thus, LifePoint's first four annual meetings were held on May 11, 2000, May 14, 2001, May 14, 2002, and May 21, 2003. That regular schedule was disrupted by various circumstances in both 2004 and 2005, when the meetings were held on June 15 and June 30, respectively.

The procedure that stockholders must follow if they wish to nominate candidates to the board of directors or to submit stockholder proposals is set forth in Section 11 of the corporation's bylaws. LifePoint's default rule is that a stockholder's proposal or nomination of directors is timely if it is delivered to the corporation "not less than 90 days prior to the first anniversary of the preceding year's annual meeting of stockholders." On those occasions where the date of the annual meeting is advanced by more than 30 days from the previous year's anniversary, or is delayed more than 60 days from that anniversary, however, a different rule applies. As set forth elsewhere in Section 11:

> If the date of the annual meeting is advanced more than 30 days prior to or delayed more than 60 days after such anniversary date, notice by the stockholder to be timely must be delivered not later than close of business on the later of the 90th day prior to such annual meeting or the 10th day following

the day on which public announcement of the date of such meeting is first made.

The bylaw further defines public announcement as "disclosure in a press release reported by the Dow Jones News Service, Associated Press or a comparable national news service or in a document publicly filed" with the SEC.

2. *The 2006 Meeting Date*

When the LifePoint board began compiling its calendar for 2006 and 2007 in the fall of 2005, the proposed date for the 2006 annual meeting was May 8, harking back to the early May annual meeting date of previous years. That initial plan was confirmed when, in mid-January 2006, LifePoint and its outside counsel prepared an annual meeting timeline that envisioned filing the company's SEC Form 10-K by February 6, at the same time LifePoint would release its earnings for the fourth quarter and year-end of 2005. The board was informally scheduled to approve the May meeting date, and the record date for the annual meeting, at a meeting on February 23, 2006. Presumably, had that schedule been adhered to, the company would have announced its annual meeting shortly thereafter.

These plans changed when LifePoint received the first stockholder proposal in its history on January 12, 2006, submitted by Amalgamated Bank LongView MidCap 400 Index Fund. The proposal was forwarded to the company's outside legal counsel, Waller Lansden Dortch & Davis, which was in the process of preparing the proxy statement for the 2006 annual meeting. On February 1, 2006, an associate at the Waller firm suggested in an internal email that LifePoint should immediately announce its annual stockholder meeting date, which would trigger LifePoint's advance notice bylaw, and require all further stockholder proposals to be submitted within 10 days of that announcement. Later, a senior partner at the firm passed the associate's suggestion to Bill Carpenter, the chief governance officer of LifePoint.

Carpenter was receptive to the idea. As he testified at his deposition, although he claimed that his goal was to "identify the universe of stockholder proposals that ... would have to be included in [LifePoint's 2006 annual] proxy statement," his preference was to receive no additional stockholder proposals. Therefore, he decided to authorize an addition to the earnings press release due to be released on February 6 to announce the May 8 annual meeting. Carpenter forthrightly testified at his deposition that he could not remember making any special effort to determine whether such proposed action complied with Delaware law or SEC regulations, but rather concentrated on complying with the terms of the company's bylaws. Nor did he remember considering whether a separate press release announcing the new date of the stockholder meeting might be more appropriate than merely adding a paragraph announcing the meeting date to the earnings release.

Acting on that authorization, Mary Kim Shipp at LifePoint wrote to the Waller firm on February 2, 2006, and explained that Carpenter wanted to "add a sentence to our earnings release that announces the date of the annual meeting in order to cut off the time for any additional shareholder proposals." Later the same day, Shipp wrote to the Waller firm again, adding that the announcement could be placed at the end of the earnings release, just before the boilerplate language preceding the financial tables. An associate at the Waller firm responded that afternoon, with sample language that omitted the fact that setting an annual meeting date in May would trigger the ten-day provision of the advance notice bylaw, and therefore set a close deadline for the submission of any further stockholder proposals. The associate explained, "[w]e don't think a deadline for shareholder proposals should be mentioned, as that would only seem to invite them." Carpenter approved the language on February 6, 2006, the very morning that the earnings release was scheduled to be sent out.[17]

3. *The February 6 Press Release and Form 8-K Filing*

LifePoint's announcement that its annual meeting would be held in May was included in the February 6 press release, which was issued publicly on that day and also filed as an attachment to a SEC Form 8-K. In both cases, the title of the document refers only to the corporation's fourth quarter and year-end results. In the format provided to the court, the press release consists of 11 pages of combined text and financial results. The first five paragraphs of the release discuss the company's improved fourth quarter and year-end 2005 results. The sixth paragraph announces the existence of a listen-only simul-cast of the company's February 7 financial results conference call with analysts. The seventh paragraph, near the bottom of the first page, is the text at issue in this case and is reproduced here in full:

> LifePoint's 2006 Annual Meeting of Stockholders will be held on May 8, 2006, at 3:00 p.m. local time, at 511 Union Street, Suite 2700, Nashville, Tennessee. The record date for the meeting will be March 17, 2006.

The eighth paragraph of the release includes only a standard description of LifePoint's business. It is followed by a sub-heading designating the text below it as "important legal information," which is followed by a long

---

[17] Although the plaintiff presents no argument as to this point, the court notes with some surprise that the record does not reflect that this decision was ever approved or ratified by LifePoint's board of directors.

paragraph of standard boilerplate disclaimers. Together, that text covers no more than a page and a half in the form presented in the evidence. The financial tables disclosing the details of LifePoint's results immediately follow, and continue for ten pages.

4. *Accipiter's Attempt to Nominate Director Candidates*

Accipiter's Hoffman and Viglucci were awaiting the February 6 earnings report and accompanying press release. Both testified that they likely read the report on or about the day it was released. Importantly, Hoffman expressly testified that if he had seen the language announcing the annual meeting when he first read the document, he would immediately have understood that Accipiter then had ten days to nominate an insurgent slate of directors:

> [H]ad I seen it, had it not been buried, had it been displayed more prominently, as is generally the case, it would have been very important and I would have seen it, I believe ... [Viglucci] and I had ... decided at least a month previously that we were definitely becoming activists ... [a]nd so something like this, considering I had read the information in the proxy prior to this ... would have triggered ... [an understanding that] we've got ten days [to make our nominations].

It is further unchallenged that had either Viglucci or Hoffman read the disclosure, and thus understood that they had ten days to make their nominations, Accipiter could have complied with that deadline. Indeed, Accipiter makes no challenge to the length of time provided by Section 11 for nominations.

Despite the separate paragraph announcing the meeting, however, both Hoffman and Viglucci claim they did not notice it. Indeed, Viglucci testified that, in accessing the financial information, she skimmed all the text up to the announcement of the webcast, skipped the one, hidden paragraph that announced the annual meeting, and continued at the financial tables that followed:

> I did not read the entire release.... I skimmed through the commentary on the financial results, however, I didn't focus on it, that's not important, it just summarizes all the financial data. I care more about looking at the actual numbers....

She attempted to explain the curious fact that even in skimming she failed to notice an entire separate paragraph announcing the corporation's annual meeting by noting that she read the announcement on a Bloomberg screen, where the text is presented in an unfriendly format, and the critical paragraph was actually on the third screen of the document.

Hoffman, for his part, testified that he could not remember reading the particular press release in question, but that he would have done so because LifePoint was a company in which Accipiter is invested, and that he would have read it on February 6, the day it was released. Hoffman explained, however, that after erroneously identifying the particular section of the press release in which the annual meeting date was disclosed as irrelevant, he likely spent most of his time reading the financial results, and thus failed to see the crucial disclosure. This was because, in his view, financial professionals cannot be expected to read every single word of every company's press release, but rather read those parts of the press release they deem relevant, and skip those they recognize as unimportant to their goals.

The defendant does not challenge either Hoffman's or Viglucci's veracity, which is supported by documents produced as part of the record.[29] The court must take as true, therefore, that both of these highly experienced financial analysts simply did not read the text of the February 6 press release in full, and thus remained ignorant until April that the annual meeting date had been set.

Unaware of the new meeting date and thus also unaware of the fact that the time for making director nominations had run, in mid-March 2006 Hoffman and Viglucci embarked on nominating a slate of director candidates. They retained a proxy solicitor and outside counsel, and set out their concerns about LifePoint's management in a letter from Hoffman to LifePoint dated March 24, 2006. Accipiter assembled a slate of nominees and submitted a formal notice of nominations to LifePoint on March 31, 2006. Accipiter issued its nomination letter as a press release on the morning of April 4, 2006. On April 4, 2006, Carpenter faxed a letter to Accipiter stating that its notice of nomination of candidates was not "timely delivered to LifePoint," based on the new annual meeting date set out in the February 6 press release. Accipiter filed suit on April 10, 2005. On April 25, 2006, this court denied Accipiter's request for preliminary injunctive relief noting the availability of speedy equitable relief.

II.

The plaintiff's case revolves, as noted above, around LifePoint's February 6 press release. In Accipiter's view, by late January 2006, LifePoint was beset by poor earnings and dissatisfied stockholders. When it received the Amalgamated stockholder proposal, LifePoint's management decided to foreclose any further attempts by stockholders to assert power over the ailing company by triggering

---

[29] The record shows that Hoffman and Viglucci were apparently surprised to discover in April that the nomination period had already run.

the advance notice bylaw in as obscure a way as possible while still formally complying with its responsibilities under the bylaws to announce its plans publicly. Accordingly, LifePoint chose to "bury" the announcement in the seventh paragraph of a purportedly 34-page (when viewed on a Bloomberg screen) press release, strategically placing this crucial information in the midst of boilerplate legal text, and in any case just before vital financial results on which LifePoint knew stockholders would concentrate their efforts.

That this was LifePoint's goal, Accipiter argues, is plainly evidenced by Shipp's and Carpenter's communications with their outside counsel, which show LifePoint's care to place the annual meeting announcement "at the end" of the earnings announcement, show LifePoint's clear desire to foreclose further stockholder proposals, and show that Carpenter undertook no due diligence to ensure that what he was doing complied with federal and state laws. In Accipiter's view, LifePoint could have announced its meeting in any number of other ways: by a separate press release, or by including the announcement of the annual meeting in the headline of the press release or in the caption of the Form 8-K. Rather than take those easy steps, Accipiter claims that LifePoint intentionally obscured its announcement, and that its efforts succeeded when Accipiter failed to notice that ten-day window for stockholder proposals and nominations began running on February 6.

Accipiter concedes there was nothing confusing about the language of the disclosure, and concedes that, if the relevant personnel at Accipiter had seen the disclosure, they would have understood its meaning, would have immediately been aware of the need to nominate its slate within ten days, and would have been able to meet that deadline. Thus, Accipiter's claim is essentially limited to its assertion that there was something so fundamentally wrong about where and how LifePoint announced its annual meeting date that the company necessarily violated its implied duties of good faith and fair dealing, ... and, most importantly, the standard of equitable behavior set forth in *Schnell v. Chris-Craft*[35] and its progeny. Therefore, the plaintiff claims, the court should grant summary judgment in its favor, and order a new election of directors to LifePoint's board.

The defendants emphasize that no one at LifePoint had so much as heard of Accipiter, or knew of any potential proxy contest, before Accipiter's April announcement. Moreover, LifePoint argues that the only explanation for LifePoint's decision to announce its annual meeting on February 6 was to identify the universe of possible stockholder proposals. That is, LifePoint disclaims even the idea that Carpenter meant to cut short further stockholder proposals. Thus, the defendants argue that LifePoint can hardly be blamed if the extremely sophisticated plaintiff, with its eyes closely fixed on their company, missed an obvious announcement placed in a discrete paragraph on the first page

---

[35] 285 A.2d 437 (Del.1971).

of an important press release. On that basis, the defendants argue that no material facts remain in dispute between the parties, and that they should be granted summary judgment.

III.

The parties' post-argument supplemental letters dispute whether summary judgment is an appropriate in this case. In sum, although Accipiter believes it is entitled to summary judgment, and believed the facts of record were appropriate for relief at the preliminary injunction stage, its June 14, 2006 letter asserts that it will be able to prove at trial that Carpenter's intent was to disclose the annual meeting obscurely, so as to escape the notice of stockholders. Accipiter believes that this allegation, which LifePoint disputes, is a material fact at issue precluding summary judgment in favor of LifePoint.

The court agrees with Accipiter that it cannot conclude, at this stage, that Carpenter's motivation was benign. On the contrary, the facts of record clearly evidence Carpenter's desire to avoid further stockholder proposals, and show that his advisors suggested including the annual meeting date in the February 6 press release for that very purpose. In that context, LifePoint's claim that Carpenter acted only to define the universe of possible proposals cannot form the basis for a summary judgment. Nonetheless, there is no evidence in the record to support the further inference that the actual language used to disclose the meeting date, the placement of that disclosure in the earnings release, or the absence of headings or captions was part of a plan to make the announcement so obscure as to escape all attention. On the contrary, the disclosure conveys the required information in plain English, in simple declarative sentences, and in a separate paragraph on the first page of an important press release. Similarly, there is no evidence that either Carpenter or anyone else actively chose to omit mention of the meeting date from the caption of either the press release or the Form 8-K. Rather, what the undisputed record shows is that the Form 8-K and the February 6 press release were already drafted when LifePoint's counsel raised the possibility of including the annual meeting announcement in the press release. When Carpenter approved that action in order to limit stockholder proposals, the critical extra paragraph was hastily inserted into the already prepared text. In the circumstances, there is no material issue of fact regarding Carpenter's state of mind that would preclude entry of summary judgment.

IV.

As to the plaintiff's claim that LifePoint violated its implied covenant of good faith and fair dealing, that assertion adds nothing to Accipiter's claims in equity. As this court has observed, "the contract doctrine of an implied covenant of good faith and fair dealing may be thought in some ways to function analogously to the fiduciary concept."[39] Given the cases discussed below, that analogy is particularly strong here.

This leaves the plaintiff's argument on equitable grounds. There is, of course, no dispute as to the plaintiff's fundamental point. Delaware corporations may not take actions towards their stockholders which, though legally possible, are inequitable. The source of that standard is *Schnell v. Chris-Craft,* where the Supreme Court held that a board's facially legal use of a bylaw to cut short the time available for stockholders to conduct a proxy contest was inequitable, and thus impermissible. That precedent is a cornerstone of Delaware law, and has repeatedly been reaffirmed by our courts.

As this court has held, however, the equitable power to set aside a board's action under *Schnell* "must be invoked sparingly and only when circumstances make relatively clear that inequitable behavior or manipulation is present."[42] As the Supreme Court has cautioned in holding that equitable principles are distinct from rights under statutory appraisal:

> While [*Schnell*] is an important part of our jurisprudence, its application, or that of similar concepts, should be reserved for those instances that threaten the fabric of the law, or which by an improper manipulation of the law, would deprive a person of a clear right.[43]

In the specific context of advance notice bylaws, *Schnell* has been understood to mean that such bylaws must on their face and in the particular circumstances "afford the shareholders a fair opportunity to nominate candidates."[44] This matter of "basic fairness" requires relief where inequitable conduct "interferes with a fair voting process."[45]

In deciding whether an act is an inequitable restraint on the stockholder's franchise, this court has looked closely at the circumstances of each case. Obviously, our courts have been more likely to find an action impermissible if the board acted with the intent of influencing or precluding a proxy contest for control of the corporation. Thus, in *Schnell* itself, there was no

---

[39] *HB Korenvaes v. Marriott Corp.,* 1993 WL 205040, *6, 1993 Del.Ch. LEXIS 90, *17 (Del.Ch. June 9, 1993).

[42] *Dolgoff v. Projectavision, Inc.,* 1996 WL 91945, *7, 1996 Del.Ch. LEXIS 24, *23 (Del.Ch. Feb. 29, 1996).

[43] *Alabama By-Products Corp. v. Neal,* 588 A.2d 255, 258 n. 1 (Del.1991).

[44] *Hubbard v. Hollywood Park Realty Enters.,* 1991 WL 3151, *11, 1991 Del.Ch. LEXIS 9, *35 (Del.Ch. Jan. 14, 1991).

[45] *Linton v. Everett,* 1997 WL 441189, *9, 1997 Del.Ch. LEXIS 117, *11 (Del.Ch. July 31, 1997).

doubt that the board acted in the face of an SEC filing declaring the proxy group's intention to nominate directors. And in *Lerman v. Diagnostic Data, Inc.,*[47]the court emphasized in its decision to invalidate the setting of an annual meeting the fact that the board acted with "full knowledge of [the dissident's] intentions" to launch a proxy contest. Other important cases in the *Schnell* line also depended in some part on the fact that the board acted with the intention of maintaining control of the corporation.[49] In *Aprahamian v. HBO & Co.,*[50]for example, this court granted relief where the board decided to postpone the annual stockholders meeting only *after* discovering that it was likely to lose a proxy contest.

None of this is to say that relief from an inequitable bylaw is dependent on a finding of scienter. In *Linton v. Everett,* for example, this court observed that intent was not necessarily a part of a claim under *Schnell:* "to set aside election results on the basis of inequitable manipulation of the corporate machinery, it is not required that scienter, i.e., actual subjective intent to impede the voting process, be shown."[52] The reason that neither knowledge of an impending proxy contest nor scienter was necessary in *Linton,* however, was that the facts at issue there were quite extraordinary.

To summarize those "highly unusual" circumstances, the *Linton* court was confronted with a situation where a corporation had not held an annual meeting in three years. When the board did finally call a meeting to elect all three classes of directors, as it was required to do under Delaware law, it triggered the company's advance notice bylaw. That provision required stockholders wishing to make director nominations to provide notice of their intentions within ten days of the mailing of the notice of the meeting. But the plaintiff stockholders testified that they had only received their mailed notice three days before the deadline. Thus, as the court observed, the only way the stockholders could have participated in the highly important election for control of the corporation was to have maintained a full slate of directors ready to be nominated on a hair trigger, on the off chance that at any moment in three years of inactivity, the corporation might call its statutorily required meeting. The unreasonableness of that requirement, as the court explained, "constituted an inequitable manipulation of the election process."

---

[47] 421 A.2d 906 (Del.Ch.1980).

[49] *See also Hubbard,* 1991 WL 3151, 1991 Del.Ch. LEXIS at 9. Although the issue in *Hubbard* turned, as discussed herein, on the fact that a material change had occurred in the company's strategic plan after the deadline imposed by an advance notice bylaw, part of the court's holding in that case centered around the fact that the company had twice used its advance notice bylaw in the context of known proxy contests. *Id.* at *2-3, 1991 Del.Ch. LEXIS at *8-9.

[50] 531 A.2d 1204 (Del.Ch.1987).

[52] 1997 WL 441189, at *9, 1997 Del.Ch. LEXIS 117, at *29.

All the other cases on which the plaintiff relies, and which constitute the chief progeny of *Schnell,* were based on similarly extraordinary facts. In *Hubbard,* for example, the chief reason that the advance notice bylaw at issue was found to be inequitable was that after the nomination deadline had passed, the leading dissident agreed to join the board, abandoned its proxy contest, and succeeded in radically changing the board's strategic plan. Thus, the court observed, the key facts on which a stockholder could choose to nominate candidates were "inherently unknowable until after the nomination deadline had expired." And in *Lerman* a court granted relief where a sitting board of directors set the annual meeting at a time 63 days in the future, in the face of a bylaw that required a stockholder wishing to nominate directors to submit the names of its nominees at least 70 days in advance of the meeting. Thus, the board's action made compliance with the bylaw literally impossible, depriving the stockholders of any access to the ballot. In these and the other cases discussed herein, it was well within this court's equitable power to provide the stockholders with relief.

The facts in this case fall far short of the types of inequity which our courts have found determinative in the past. Most obviously, this case differs entirely from most of our previous cases on point because no one at LifePoint had reason to know of Accipiter's intention to trigger a proxy contest when Carpenter made the decision to announce the company's annual meeting. Unlike *Aprahamian,* or *Schnell,* or *Lerman,* the defendants here did not act with the specific intent to limit the stockholder's rights to nominate and elect a dissident slate. Rather, as in *Dolgoff,* "the board was not faced with a proxy contest or an expected proxy contest when it took action," nor did it "advance or delay the meeting after it had already been called."[58] To the extent that Carpenter's intent to limit stockholder proposals is relevant to the court's conclusion, the analysis below—finding that LifePoint's actions are not of the gravity forbidden by *Schnell*—is determinative.

The gravamen of Accipiter's case is that the form of LifePoint's annual meeting announcement violated Delaware law by making important corporate information more difficult to discover than was necessary. There is some appeal to that argument resulting from the sense of discomfort the February 6 press release engenders. Clearly, the annual meeting announcement would have been completely unmistakable had LifePoint specifically included it in the caption of either the press release or the Form 8-K, or had it issued a separate press release to that effect. Even a separate subheading in the press release alerting readers to the additional topic would have considerably improved the quality of LifePoint's disclosure.

Thus, the court shares Accipiter's concerns about the manner and form of LifePoint's annual meeting announcement. Further, this court does not lightly

---

[58] *Dolgoff v. Projectavision, Inc.,* 1996 WL 91945, at *8, 1996 Del.Ch. LEXIS 24, at *24-25 (Del.Ch. Feb. 29, 1996).

approve a process which was intended to limit the rights of some stockholders, and which had the incidental, and indirect, effect of precluding a contested election for the board. While this case has some of the hallmarks of the *Schnell* line of cases, however, LifePoint's concededly troubling way of announcing its annual meeting does not reach the standard required for equitable relief. LifePoint's actions did not, as in *Linton* or *Schnell,* make the dissident's challenge extremely difficult or impossible. Nor did material facts arise after the nomination period ended, as in *Hubbard.* Importantly, unlike the cases detailed above, all Accipiter needed to do to preserve its rights was read the company's press release carefully and in full. This is in contrast to *Lerman,* for example, where in order to preserve its rights to nominate directors, the dissident stockholder would have had to anticipate that the company would call its annual meeting in a way that would make further nominations impossible. As this court rightly held in *Hubbard,* where the defendant went so far as to claim that the plaintiff should have anticipated that the initial dissident might seek an accommodation with the board, and thus deprive a second set of dissidents of a contested election, stockholders are not required to be clairvoyant. The burden LifePoint's announcement placed on Accipiter, however, was not of this kind.

The reason this court grants the defendants' motion for summary judgment, therefore, is not that the court views LifePoint's method of disclosure with approbation, but that its equitable powers can only be roused under *Schnell* where compelling circumstances suggest that the company unfairly manipulated the voting process in such a serious way as to constitute an evident or grave incursion into the fabric of the corporate law. To rule in the plaintiff's favor here, where the record shows that Accipiter could easily have preserved its rights with reasonable diligence, would extend *Schnell* well beyond those limits and would threaten to involve the court in matters better understood as regulatory in nature. The rules the court would arrive at, exercising such regulatory oversight, might, on occasion, be wise. And yet, such rulemaking is inconsistent with precedent, and with this court's limited powers in equity to prevent the deprivation of a clear right by improper manipulation.

V.

For the foregoing reasons, the defendants' motion for summary judgment is GRANTED.

Notes and Questions

1. Reality Check

a. What LifePoint actions is the plaintiff challenging?

b. Did LifePoint violate the DGCL, its Certificate of Incorporation, or its bylaws? If not, what is the basis of Accipiter's challenge?

c. Why did LifePoint prevail?

d. What legal rules does Vice Chancellor Lamb use?

e. How did Vice Chancellor Lamb apply the rules to the facts?

f. Why did LifePoint want to hide its announcement of the annual meeting?

g. How was Accipiter hurt by LifePoint's actions? Was any other person or entity harmed?

h. Did LifePoint intend to harm Accipter or other shareholders?

i. What role was played by LifePoint's directors and senior managers? By in-house counsel? By outside counsel?

2. Suppose

a. Suppose that Mr. Hoffman and Ms. Viglucci had never read the press release at all. Would the court's analysis or the result be different?

3. What Do You Think?

a. Would Accipiter have been better off had Mr. Hoffman and Ms. Viglucci never read the press release at all? If so, does the court's reasoning or the result make sense?

b. Is there a moral or an ethical dimension to LifePoint's actions or those of its lawyers? If so, is it a problem that implicates the Rules of Professional Conduct?

c. Is this case fundamentally similar to, or fundamentally different from, *McKesson Corp. v. Derdiger* on casebook page 546?

d. What should LifePoint and its advisors have done after receiving the shareholder proposal?

e. Do you think LifePoint's motivation was proper in relation to its stockholders?

Page 555

Add the following before "**v. The Importance of Being Present**", which will be renumbered in the second edition:

v. The Simple Majority Vote Movement. In publicly held corporations, the nominating committee of the board recommends candidates for director positions. Current directors whose terms are expiring are typically re-nominated. The candidates nominated by the board will be elected easily. This is so for at least two reasons. First, the shares of most public corporations are sufficiently diffused that proponents of other candidates will not realistically be able to garner enough votes to defeat the board's candidates. Second, recall that directors are elected by a plurality. That corporate law rule means that any other vote than "for" would have no effect; it is only the number of "for" votes that matter. One shareholder owning a single share would elect the entire board simply by voting "yes" for the board's nominees, even if every other shareholder voted "withhold" for every board candidate.

In some instances, however, dissident shareholders have enough resources to wage a *proxy fight*, which is an attempt to replace the current directors, or the board-nominated candidates, by fielding an alternative slate of board candidates and soliciting proxies from the shareholders. Proxy fights are expensive and are rarely undertaken except by a party interested in acquiring the entire corporation.

Beginning with the corporate scandals at the millennium (see Chapter 14), many mutual funds and pension funds, who typically are large shareholders in public companies, began to demonstrate their frustration with, and disapproval of, corporate managers by withholding their votes for directors. This movement was, of course, symbolic rather than effective. Then, in 2004, the pension fund of a labor union, the United Brotherhood of Carpenters and Joiners of America, started a campaign to change the plurality rule. This campaign has become known as the *simple majority vote movement.*

The success of the simple majority vote movement has been astonishing. Within three years of the start of the campaign, about one third of the largest public corporations provide that directors shall be elected by a simple majority vote. In early 2006 Intel Corporation became the first prominent public corporation to accede to this movement.

In brief, the simple majority vote movement seeks to persuade public companies to require a simple majority vote (i.e., a majority of the votes cast) to elect directors. As a matter of corporate law, the shift from the plurality standard to the simple majority standard is accomplished through a bylaw provision. Intel's bylaw reads,

[E]ach director shall be elected by the vote of the majority of the votes cast with respect to the director at any meeting for the election of directors at which a quorum is present ....

For purposes of this Section, a majority of the votes cast means that the number of shares voted "for" a director must exceed the number of votes cast against that director.

Even with a simple majority vote standard, in the publicly held corporation it will be extraordinary for a board candidate to be defeated. Nonetheless, activist shareholders view the simple majority vote movement as an important victory for shareholder rights.

What happens when a board-nominated candidate does not receive a simple majority of votes? The result, of course, is not a vacancy but a holdover director. In the vast majority of cases, the non-elected candidate *is* the holdover. Under corporate law, failing to be re-elected is not the same as being removed. Further, many corporations limit removal of directors to removal for cause, which would not include failing to be re-elected, without more. This would result in a pyrrhic victory for the shareholders who successfully prevented the election of a director.

In light of the holdover director rule, the proponents of the simple majority vote movement have pushed for adoption of a bylaw that circumvents the holdover rule. The result is that corporations that adopt a simple majority vote bylaw also usually require that all directors, as a condition of being nominated by the board for another term, submit an irrevocable resignation that becomes effective if they do not receive a simple majority of votes. The resignation creates a vacancy that is then filled by the remaining board members but obviously cannot be filled by the just-resigned director.

Considerable uncertainty surrounded majority vote bylaws and mandatory contingent irrevocable resignations. One question was whether the board could repeal the simple majority vote bylaw without shareholder approval. Another question was whether a simple majority provision could be in the bylaws rather than in the articles, which are more cumbersome to amend. A third uncertainty was that the resignation provisions, which are imposed by the board itself, could be construed as a de facto director removal provision, which would violate the statutory requirement that only the stockholders may remove a director. See DGCL § 141(k), MBCA § 8.08. On a practical level, it was unclear whether the board or shareholders would have any recourse against a director who refused to resign or who revoked his or her resignation.

Both Delaware and the Model Act have been amended to clarify these uncertainties. Under both statutes, bylaws may change the plurality default rule for electing directors and, if adopted by the shareholders, may not be changed by the board. Both statutes also permit a director resignation to be contingent on the result of a shareholder vote and permit such a contingent resignation to be irrevocable. See DGCL §§ 141(b), 216 and MBCA §§ 8.05, 8.07, and 10.22.

We spoke earlier about proxy fights, wherein a group wages a campaign to gain control of the board. The simple majority vote proponents do not wish to gain control of corporations. They want to make it easier to oust particular directors. In a political compromise between the simple majority vote proponents and corporate boards, the statutes provide that simple majority vote and contingent irrevocable resignation provisions need not apply in a proxy fight.

Page 558

Add the following before "**3. How Shareholders Take Action by Consent in Lieu of a Meeting**":

Erin White, *Stage-Managing the Annual Meeting*
Wall St. J. (Apr. 16, 2007)

At last year's annual meeting of restaurant operator Brinker International Inc., shareholder activist Matt Prescott noticed a man following him everywhere—even into the bathroom. "He was my own personal escort," quips Mr. Prescott, a manager at People for the Ethical Treatment of Animals, who was pressing the operator of Chili's and Macaroni Grill for a report on suppliers' slaughter methods.

As shareholder activists turn up the heat on corporate officials at annual meetings, officials seek inventive ways to stage-manage the events and defuse potential controversies. Some tactics: assign minders to activists; require questions to be submitted in writing; enforce time limits on speakers; and use stationary rather than roving microphones, creating a more orderly atmosphere.

Annual meetings can become a "circus environment," says Ron Culp of public-relations firm Ketchum, which advises companies on conducting the meetings. He says many chief executive officers would "rather be in a dentist's chair."

Companies must be deft in their stage management, lest the efforts backfire. Wal-Mart Stores Inc. this month apologized to some shareholders after a report that the company had sought to investigate the sponsors of shareholder resolutions.

Public-relations advisers say it's normal for companies to do some premeeting research, often using the Google search engine or conducting newspaper clip searches on shareholder sponsors. In the Wal-Mart case, however, New York City's comptroller has asked government officials to investigate.

Outside directors of Home Depot Inc. faced stinging criticism last year after they skipped the retailer's annual meeting. (In a statement at the time, the

company said "many" directors were at headquarters "on company business.")
This year, shareholder activists plan to confront executives and directors where
they believe executives are overpaid.

Some companies seek to avoid problems at annual meetings by
consulting with shareholders or intermediaries beforehand. Last year, slot-
machine maker WMS Industries Inc. revised a proposed employee stock and
stock-option plan after discussions with proxy adviser Institutional Shareholder
Services, according to Kathleen McJohn, WMS's general counsel. The plan
passed, with no questions at the annual meeting.

Others take a more confrontational approach. At Home Depot's
meeting in Wilmington, Del., last year, several dozen beefy on-staff "greeters"
wearing orange store aprons nearly outnumbered nonemployee shareholders,
says Richard Ferlauto, director of pension-investment policy at the American
Federation of State, County and Municipal Employees. Sponsors of shareholder
resolutions were allocated three minutes to speak; other items were limited to
one minute.

Mr. Ferlauto rose at one point to object to directors' absence. When his
one minute was up, a pair of greeters took positions on either side of him at the
microphone. "They were intimidating enough that when they said, 'Your time is
over,' I stopped talking," Mr. Ferlauto remembers. "It was definitely an
orchestrated attempt to manage the meeting with big guys."

Home Depot declined to comment on Mr. Ferlauto's experience and
referred to a statement issued last year, in which the company pledged to return
"to our traditional format" and that directors would attend this year's meeting,
scheduled for May 24 in Atlanta.

Mr. Ferlauto recalls a similar experience at the 2003 annual meeting for
Ingersoll-Rand Co. He had submitted a resolution asking the company to move
its incorporation back to the U.S. from Bermuda. Arriving at the meeting, in an
Ingersoll manufacturing and training facility in Davidson, N.C., Mr. Ferlauto
says he was met by an investor-relations official, who showed him to his seat,
sat beside him during the meeting and walked him out the door afterward. Media
weren't invited. Paul Dickard, an Ingersoll spokesman, says the company
wanted to reserve the meeting for shareholders. Mr. Dickard says he has no
knowledge of any escort. "We're not trying to control what people do or say,"
he says.

At the Brinker meeting last year in Dallas, Mr. Prescott spoke in
support of a PETA resolution asking the company to report on suppliers' use of
what PETA believes is a more humane slaughter method. He says a company
official cut him off before his allotted time was up. (Brinker didn't respond to
requests for comment.)

Mr. Prescott says he faced different tactics at the meeting in February
of Jack in the Box Inc., another restaurant operator. The company requested that
shareholders submit written questions, which were then read by a company

official. Brian Luscomb, a company spokesman, says the policy is "a way to keep the meeting focused on the agenda."

Mr. Prescott submitted a question about suppliers' treatment of animals that included a graphic description of slaughter methods. When the question was read aloud, the speaker phrased it as a generic question about animal welfare, Mr. Prescott says. Mr. Luscomb says a senior vice president fully answered the question; Mr. Prescott disagrees.

Other companies hold their meetings in unconventional locations, which some shareholders suspect–but the companies deny–is an effort to minimize attendance and disruption. In 1990 U-Haul's parent company, Amerco of Reno, Nev., held its annual meeting in Tonopah, Nev., population 2,627. Jennifer Flachman, director of investor relations, says the location was selected because it was a convenient halfway point between U-Haul's founders' home in Las Vegas and Amerco's offices in Reno. Also, Ms. Flachman notes, the venue was a bargain.

Last year, New York pharmaceutical giant Pfizer Inc. held its annual meeting in Lincoln, Neb. Pfizer says it rotates meeting locations to major operations sites, including a manufacturing facility in Lincoln, so directors can see operations first-hand and people across the country may attend. (The location far from New York didn't deter controversy over the size of then-CEO Henry McKinnell's projected retirement package.)

Firms with a history of placid annual meetings say showing courtesy to shareholders can generate goodwill. When faced with the occasional speech-making shareholder, for instance, Pitney Bowes Inc. Chairman Michael Critelli is "unrelentingly polite," says Amy Corn, corporate secretary. Mr. Ferlauto of AFSCME, which submitted a resolution in 2003, agrees the group has a "very cordial relationship" with Pitney Bowes, a maker of postage meters and other mailing devices.

One year, an elderly woman in the audience began reading a long speech in support of an environmental resolution; she looked flustered with her papers. Mr. Critelli asked if she would be more comfortable on stage, where she could place her papers on the podium. She agreed, and finished her speech. The proposal didn't pass. "We have pretty quiet meetings," Ms. Corn says.

Page 558

MBCA § 7.04 has been amended to provide for shareholder action by non-unanimous written consent in lieu of a meeting.

In the fifth paragraph omit "Under the MBCA, shareholder action without a meeting must be unanimous, which obviously limits such provisions to closely held corporations where the shareholders are of a single mind. See MBCA § 7.04."

Pages 558-559

The MBCA § 7.04 has been amended to provide for shareholder action by non-unanimous written consent in lieu of a meeting.
In the final paragraph on page 558 and the first two paragraphs on page 559, add a citation to MBCA § 7.04 after each citation to the DGCL.

Page 567

Replace *Compaq Computer Corp. v. Horton* with:

Seinfeld v. Verizon Communications, Inc.
909 A.2d 117 (Del. 2006)

HOLLAND, J.

The plaintiff-appellant, Frank D. Seinfeld ("Seinfeld"), brought suit under section 220 of the Delaware General Corporation Law to compel the defendant-appellee, Verizon Communications, Inc. ("Verizon"), to produce, for his inspection, its books and records related to the compensation of Verizon's three highest corporate officers from 2000 to 2002. Seinfeld claimed that their executive compensation, individually and collectively, was excessive and wasteful. On cross-motions for summary judgment, the Court of Chancery applied well-established Delaware law and held that Seinfeld had not met his evidentiary burden to demonstrate a proper purpose to justify the inspection of Verizon's records.

Facts

Seinfeld asserts that he is the beneficial owner of approximately 3,884 shares of Verizon, held in street name through a brokerage firm. His stated purpose for seeking Verizon's books and records was to investigate mismanagement and corporate waste regarding the executive compensations of Ivan G. Seidenberg, Lawrence T. Babbio, Jr. and Charles R. Lee. Seinfeld alleges that the three executives were all performing in the same job and were paid amounts, including stock options, above the compensation provided for in their employment contracts. Seinfeld's section 220 claim for inspection is further premised on various computations he performed which indicate that the three executives' compensation totaled $205 million over three years and was, therefore, excessive, given their responsibilities to the corporation.

During his deposition, Seinfeld acknowledged he had no factual support for his claim that mismanagement had taken place. He admitted that the three executives did not perform any duplicative work. Seinfeld conceded he had no factual basis to allege the executives "did not earn" the amounts paid to them under their respective employment agreements. Seinfeld also admitted "there is a possibility" that the $205 million executive compensation amount he calculated was wrong.

The issue before us is quite narrow: should a stockholder seeking inspection under section 220 be entitled to relief without being required to show some evidence to suggest a credible basis for wrongdoing? We conclude that the answer must be no.

Stockholder Inspection Rights

Delaware corporate law provides for a separation of legal control and ownership. The legal responsibility to manage the business of the corporation for the benefit of the stockholder owners is conferred on the board of directors by statute. The common law imposes fiduciary duties upon the directors of Delaware corporations to constrain their conduct when discharging that statutory responsibility.

Stockholders' rights to inspect the corporation's books and records were recognized at common law because "[a]s a matter of self-protection, the stockholder was entitled to know how his agents were conducting the affairs of the corporation of which he or she was a part owner."[8] The qualified inspection rights that originated at common law are now codified in [DGCL] 220 ....

Section 220 provides stockholders of Delaware corporations with a "powerful right."[9] By properly asserting that right under section 220, stockholders are able to obtain information that can be used in a variety of contexts. Stockholders may use information about corporate mismanagement, waste or wrongdoing in several ways. For example, they may: institute derivative litigation; "seek an audience with the board [of directors] to discuss proposed reform or, failing in that, they may prepare a stockholder resolution for the next annual meeting, or mount a proxy fight to elect new directors."[10]

Inspection Litigation Increases

More than a decade ago, we noted that "[s]urprisingly, little use has been made of section 220 as an information-gathering tool in the derivative [suit]

---

[8] *Saito v. McKesson HBOC, Inc.*, 806 A.2d 113, 116 (Del.2002) (citing *Shaw v. Agri-Mark, Inc.*, 663 A.2d 464, 467 (Del.1995)).

[9] *Disney v. Walt Disney Co.*, 857 A.2d 444, 447 (Del.Ch.2004).

[10] *Saito v. McKesson HBOC, Inc.*, 806 A.2d at 117.

context."[11] Today, however, stockholders who have concerns about corporate governance are increasingly making a broad array of section 220 demands. The rise in books and records litigation is directly attributable to this Court's encouragement of stockholders, who can show a proper purpose, to use the "tools at hand" to obtain the necessary information before filing a derivative action.[13] Section 220 is now recognized as "an important part of the corporate governance landscape."[14]

Seinfeld Denied Inspection

The Court of Chancery determined that Seinfeld's deposition testimony established only that he was concerned about the large amount of compensation paid to the three executives. That court concluded that Seinfeld offered "no evidence from which [it] could evaluate whether there is a reasonable ground for suspicion that the executive's compensation rises to the level of waste." It also concluded that Seinfeld did not "submit any evidence showing that the executives were not entitled to [the stock] options." The Court of Chancery properly noted that a disagreement with the business judgment of Verizon's board of directors or its compensation committee is not evidence of wrongdoing and did not satisfy Seinfeld's burden under section 220.

Evidentiary Barrier Allegation

In this appeal, Seinfeld asserts that the "Court of Chancery's ruling erects an insurmountable barrier for the minority shareholder of a public company." Seinfeld argues that:

> This Court and the Court of Chancery have instructed shareholders to utilize § 220 as one of the tools at hand. Yet, the Court of Chancery at bar, in requiring *evidence* makes a § 220 application a mirage. If the shareholder had evidence, a derivative suit would be brought. Unless there is a whistle blower, or a video

---

[11] *Rales v. Blasband,* 634 A.2d 927, 934-35 n. 10 (Del.1993) (quoted in *Grimes v. Donald,* 673 A.2d 1207, 1216 n. 11 (Del.1996)).

[13] *Grimes v. Donald,* 673 A.2d at 1216 (citing *Rales v. Blasband,* 634 A.2d at 934-35 n. 10). *See also Beam ex rel. Martha Stewart Living Omnimedia, Inc. v. Stewart,* 833 A.2d 961, 981 nn. 65-66 (Del.Ch.2003) (collecting cases).

[14] *Security First Corp. v. U.S. Die Casting & Dev. Co.,* 687 A.2d 563, 571 (Del.1997). *See also* E. Norman Veasey & Christine T. DiGuglielmo, *What Happened in Delaware Corporate Law and Governance from 1992-2004? A Retrospective on Some Key Developments,* 153 U. Pa. L.Rev. 1399, 1466-69 (2005) (discussing the use of section 220 and cases that have applied it).

cassette, the public shareholder, having no access to corporate records, will only have suspicions.

Seinfeld submits that "by requiring evidence, the shareholder is prevented from using the tools at hand." Seinfeld's brief concludes with a request for this Court to reduce the burden of proof that stockholders must meet in a section 220 action:

> Plaintiff submits that in a case involving public companies, minority shareholders who have access only to public documents and without a whistle blower or corporate documents should be permitted to have limited inspection based upon suspicions, reasonable beliefs, and logic arising from public disclosures.

After oral arguments, this Court asked the parties for supplemental briefs that would address the following questions:

> A. Should a stockholder with a proper purpose be entitled to inspect carefully limited categories of corporate books and records, pursuant to Section 220, upon a showing that the stockholder has a rational basis for the stated purpose and no other purpose that would militate against inspection?

> B. If the standard in question "A" would not be appropriate, is there *any* reduced burden of proof under Section 220 that would improve stockholders' ability to obtain the "tools" to pursue derivative claims without disrupting corporations' orderly conduct of business and without inappropriately interfering with corporate decision-making? If so, articulate the reduced burden of proof. If not, explain why not.

We asked these questions in order to review the current balance between the rights of stockholders and corporations that is established by *Thomas & Betts Corp. v. Leviton Mfg. Co.*[22] and *Security First Corp. v. U.S. Die Casting & Dev. Co.*[23] and their progeny.

Credible Basis from Some Evidence

In a section 220 action, a stockholder has the burden of proof to demonstrate a proper purpose by a preponderance of the evidence. It is well established that a stockholder's desire to investigate wrongdoing or mismanagement is a "proper

---

[22] *Thomas & Betts Corp. v. Leviton Mfg. Co.*, 681 A.2d 1026, 1031 (Del.1996).

[23] *Security First Corp. v. U.S. Die Casting & Dev. Co.*, 687 A.2d 563 (Del.1997).

purpose." Such investigations are proper, because where the allegations of mismanagement prove meritorious, investigation furthers the interest of all stockholders and should increase stockholder return.[26]

The evolution of Delaware's jurisprudence in section 220 actions reflects judicial efforts to maintain a proper balance between the rights of shareholders to obtain information based upon credible allegations of corporation mismanagement and the rights of directors to manage the business of the corporation without undue interference from stockholders. In *Thomas & Betts,* this Court held that, to meet its "burden of proof, a stockholder must present some *credible basis* from which the court can infer that waste or mismanagement may have occurred."[27] Six months later, in *Security First,* this Court held "[t]here must be *some evidence* of possible mismanagement as would warrant further investigation of the matter."[28]

Our holdings in *Thomas & Betts* and *Security First* were contemporaneous with our decisions that initially encouraged stockholders to make greater use of section 220. In *Grimes v. Donald,* decided just months before *Thomas & Betts,* this Court reaffirmed the salutary use of section 220 as one of the "tools at hand" for stockholders to use to obtain information. When the plaintiff in *Thomas & Betts* suggested that the burden of demonstrating a proper purpose had been attenuated by our encouragement for stockholders to use section 220, we rejected that argument:

> Contrary to plaintiff's assertion in the instant case, this Court in *Grimes* did not suggest that its reference to a Section 220 demand as one of the "tools at hand" was intended to eviscerate or modify the need for a stockholder to show a proper purpose under Section 220.[30]

In *Security First* and *Thomas & Betts*, we adhered to the Court of Chancery's holding in *Helmsman Mgmt. Servs., Inc. v. A & S Consultants, Inc.* that:

---

[26] *See Saito v. McKesson HBOC, Inc.,* 806 A.2d 113, 115 (Del.2002) ("where a [section] 220 claim is based on alleged corporate wrongdoing, and assuming the allegation is meritorious, the stockholder should be given enough information to effectively address the problem, either through derivative litigation or through direct contact with the corporation's directors and/or stockholders").

[27] *Thomas & Betts Corp. v. Leviton Mfg. Co.,* 681 A.2d at 1031 (emphasis added).

[28] *Security First Corp. v. U.S. Die Casting & Dev. Co.,* 687 A.2d at 568 (original emphasis omitted; emphasis added) (quoting *Helmsman Mgmt. Servs., Inc. v. A & S Consultants, Inc.,* 525 A.2d 160, 166 (Del.Ch.1987)).

[30] *Thomas & Betts Corp. v. Leviton Mfg. Co., Inc.,* 681 A.2d 1026, 1031 n. 3 (Del.1996).

A mere statement of a purpose to investigate possible general mismanagement, without more, will not entitle a shareholder to broad § 220 inspection relief. There must be *some evidence* of possible mismanagement as would warrant further investigation of the matter.[31]

Standard Achieves Balance

Investigations of meritorious allegations of possible mismanagement, waste or wrongdoing, benefit the corporation, but investigations that are "indiscriminate fishing expeditions" do not.[32] "At some point, the costs of generating more information fall short of the benefits of having more information. At that point, compelling production of information would be wealth-reducing, and so shareholders would not want it produced."[33] Accordingly, this Court has held that an inspection to investigate possible wrongdoing where there is no "credible basis," is a license for "fishing expeditions" and thus adverse to the interests of the corporation:[34]

> Stockholders have a right to at least a limited inquiry into books and records when they have established some credible basis to believe that there has been wrongdoing.... Yet it would invite mischief to open corporate management to indiscriminate fishing expeditions.[35]

A stockholder is "not required to prove by a preponderance of the evidence that waste and [mis]management are actually occurring."[36] Stockholders need only show, by a preponderance of the evidence, a credible

---

[31] *Helmsman Mgmt. Servs., Inc. v. A & S Consultants, Inc.*, 525 A.2d at 166 (emphasis added); *see also Security First Corp. v. U.S. Die Casting & Dev. Co.*, 687 A.2d at 568; *Thomas & Betts Corp. v. Leviton Mfg. Co.*, 681 A.2d at 1031.

[32] *Security First Corp. v. U.S. Die Casting & Dev. Co.*, 687 A.2d 563, 571 (Del.1997).

[33] Fred S. McChesney, *"Proper Purpose,"* Fiduciary Duties, and Shareholder-Raider Access to Corporate Information, 68 U. Cin. L.Rev. 1199, 1207-08 (2000).

[34] *Security First Corp. v. U.S. Die Casting & Dev. Co.*, 687 A.2d at 571. *See also Skouras v. Admiralty Enters., Inc.*, 386 A.2d 674, 679 (Del.Ch.1978) (noting that the use of a books and records inspection to harass the corporate defendant is improper); *Skoglund v. Ormand Indus., Inc.*, 372 A.2d 204, 210 (Del.Ch.1976) (noting that the pursuit of a fishing expedition would be improper).

[35] *Security First Corp. v. U.S. Die Casting & Dev. Co.*, 687 A.2d at 571.

[36] *Thomas & Betts Corp. v. Leviton Mfg. Co. Inc.*, 681 A.2d 1026, 1031 (Del.1996) ("In order to meet that burden of proof, a stockholder must present some credible basis from which the court can infer that waste or mismanagement may have occurred.").

basis from which the Court of Chancery can infer there is possible mismanagement that would warrant further investigation–a showing that "may ultimately fall well short of demonstrating that anything wrong occurred."[38] That "threshold may be satisfied by a credible showing, through documents, logic, testimony or otherwise, that there are legitimate issues of wrongdoing."[39]

Although the threshold for a stockholder in a section 220 proceeding is not insubstantial, the "credible basis" standard sets the lowest possible burden of proof. The only way to reduce the burden of proof further would be to eliminate any requirement that a stockholder show *some evidence* of possible wrongdoing. That would be tantamount to permitting inspection based on the "mere suspicion" standard that Seinfeld advances in this appeal. However, such a standard has been repeatedly rejected as a basis to justify the enterprise cost of an inspection.[41]

In Delaware and elsewhere,[42] the "credible-basis-from-some-evidence" standard is settled law. Under the doctrine of *stare decisis,* settled law is overruled only "for urgent reasons and upon clear manifestation of error."[43] A review of the cases that have applied the "credible basis" standard refutes Seinfeld's premise that requiring "some evidence" constitutes an insurmountable barrier for stockholders who assert inspection rights under section 220.

Requiring stockholders to establish a "credible basis" for the Court of Chancery to infer possible wrongdoing by presenting "some evidence" has not impeded stockholder inspections. Although many section 220 proceedings have been filed since we decided *Security First* and *Thomas & Betts,* Verizon points out that Seinfeld's case is only the second proceeding in which a plaintiff's

---

[38] *Khanna v. Covad Commc'ns Group, Inc.,* 2004 WL 187274 at *6 n. 25 (Del.Ch.). *See also Forsythe v. CIBC Employee Private Equity Fund (U.S.) I.L.P.,* 2005 WL 1653963, at *5 (Del.Ch.) (finding that "[w]hile the [ ] facts fall well short of actually proving wrongdoing, they do provide a credible basis for inferring mismanagement").

[39] *Security First Corp. v. U.S. Die Casting & Dev. Co.,* 687 A.2d at 568.

[41] *E.g., White v. Panic,* 783 A.2d 543, 557 n. 54 (Del.2001); *Security First Corp. v. U.S. Die Casting & Dev. Co.,* 687 A.2d at 568; *Mattes v. Checkers Drive-In Rests., Inc.,* 2001 WL 337865, at *5 (Del.Ch.); *Dobler v. Montgomery Cellular Holding Co.,* 2001 WL 1334182, at *3; *Sahagen Satellite Tech. Group, LLC v. Ellipso, Inc.,* 791 A.2d 794, 796 (Del.Ch. 2000).

[42] The "credible basis" standard is also settled law in those states that look to Delaware law for guidance on matters of corporation law. *See, e.g., Arctic Fin. Corp. v. OTR Express, Inc.,* 272 Kan. 1326, 38 P.3d 701, 703-04 (2002) (looking to *Security First* and *Thomas & Betts* for guidance regarding a books and records inspection under Kansas law); *Towle v. Robinson Springs Corp.,* 168 Vt. 226, 719 A.2d 880, 882 (1998) (in a books and records case under Vermont law, citing *Thomas & Betts* for the proposition that "[c]laims of mismanagement, however, must be supported by evidence").

[43] *Oscar George, Inc. v. Potts,* 115 A.2d 479, 481 (Del.1955).

demand to investigate wrongdoing was found to be *entirely* without a "credible basis."[44] In contrast, there are a myriad of cases where stockholders have successfully presented "some evidence" to establish a "credible basis" to infer possible mismanagement and thus received some narrowly tailored right of inspection.[45]

---

[44] *See Mattes v. Checkers Drive-In Restaurants, Inc.*, 2001 WL 337865, at *5 (Del.Ch.) (finding that "[t]he evidence at trial did not show 'a credible basis' " to support plaintiff's allegations of corporate wrongdoing when the evidence represented mere curiosity and disagreement with various business decisions and where there was a "substantial delay" in the plaintiff asserting his rights).

[45] *Sutherland v. Dardanelle Timber Co.*, 2006 WL 1451531, at *8 (Del.Ch.) (finding that the plaintiffs demonstrated a "credible basis" to support allegations of management entrenchment and waste); *Haywood v. Ambase Corp.*, 2005 WL 2130614, at *5-6 (Del.Ch.) (finding "by a preponderance of the evidence, a credible basis" to support allegations of excessive executive compensation); *Deephaven Risk Arb Trading Ltd. v. UnitedGlobalCom, Inc.*, 2005 WL 1713067, at *9-10 (Del.Ch.) (finding that the plaintiff proved "by a preponderance of the evidence a credible basis" to support allegations of mismanagement based on "sufficiently inconsistent" corporate press releases appearing to contain false or misleading information); *Forsythe v. CIBC Employee Private Equity Fund (U.S.) I.L.P.*, 2005 WL 1653963, at *5 (Del.Ch.) ("finding a credible basis for inferring mismanagement"); *Cohen v. El Paso Corp.*, 2004 WL 2340046, at *2 (Del.Ch.) ("finding that two incidents provide a credible basis upon which [the shareholder] alleges a proper purpose in investigating waste and mismanagement."); *Deephaven Risk Arb. Trading Ltd. v. UnitedGlobalCom, Inc.*, 2004 WL 1945546, at *7 (Del.Ch.) (holding that a "credible basis" was established based on the shareholder's claims); *Marathon Partners, L.P. v. M & F Worldwide Corp.*, 2004 WL 1728604, at *9 (Del.Ch.) (shareholders presented sufficient evidence to support a claim of corporate wrongdoing); *Marmon v. Arbinet-Thexchange, Inc.*, 2004 WL 936512, at *4 (Del.Ch.) (finding a "credible basis" where there was credible testimony presented in support of the various claims of corporate wrongdoing); *Khanna v. Covad Commc'ns Group, Inc.*, 2004 WL 187274, at *6 (Del.Ch.) (holding that the shareholder has shown a "credible basis" by a preponderance of the evidence for his allegations of self-dealing with respect to a number of corporate transactions); *Freund v. Lucent Technologies, Inc.*, 2003 WL 139766, at *3 (Del.Ch.) (finding "some credible basis" for an inspection pursuant to claims of corporate waste and mismanagement); *Magid v. Acceptance Ins. Cos., Inc.*, 2001 WL 1497177, at *3 (Del.Ch.) (holding that expert testimony provided a "credible basis" from which a court could infer that corporate wrongdoing took place.); *Dobler v. Montgomery Cellular Holding Co., Inc.*, 2001 WL 1334182, at *4 (Del.Ch.) (holding that the plaintiff-shareholders demonstrated a "credible basis" for its § 220 claim "[t]hrough the testimony of their two trial witnesses and the documents introduced as evidence" regarding the actions of the corporation's board of directors, through evidence of suspicious expense figures); *Saito v. McKesson HBOC, Inc.*, 2001 WL 818173, at *4 (Del.Ch.), *aff'd in part, rev'd in part on other grounds*, 806 A.2d 113 (Del.2002) (finding a "credible basis" for wrongdoing where the corporation restated its financials and federal authorities commenced criminal proceedings); *Carapico v. Phila. Stock Exch. Inc.*, 791 A.2d 787, 792 (Del.Ch.2000) (finding a "credible basis" to support an investigation of corporate mismanagement where misconduct was identified in an SEC Order and plaintiff produced testimony showing a credible basis to suspect mismanagement); *Sahagen Satellite Tech. Group, LLC v. Ellipso, Inc.*, 791 A.2d 794, 796-99 (Del.Ch.2000) (granting limited relief under the credible basis standard to allow investigation of documents related to a corporate computer purchase).

We remain convinced that the rights of stockholders and the interests of the corporation in a section 220 proceeding are properly balanced by requiring a stockholder to show "some evidence of *possible* mismanagement as would warrant further investigation."[46] The "credible basis" standard maximizes stockholder value by limiting the range of permitted stockholder inspections to those that might have merit. Accordingly, our holdings in *Security First* and *Thomas & Betts* are ratified and reaffirmed.

Conclusion

The judgment of the Court of Chancery is affirmed.

Notes and Questions

1. Reality Check

a. Why does Mr. Seinfeld want to inspect Verizon's records? What records does he want to inspect?

b. Is Mr. Seinfeld's purpose in inspecting Verizon's records a proper one? What rule does Justice Holland use to answer that question?

c. What is the current burden of proof for shareholder inspection?

d. What alternative burdens of proof are suggested? Why does the court reject them?

e. Why did Mr. Seinfeld not prevail?

2. What Do You Think?

a. Do you think the court chose the appropriate rule?

b. Why do you think the court would hear this case *en banc* if the end result was to reaffirm the long-standing rule?

c. Do you agree that the current standard is too strict, given that books and records litigation is increasing and that inspection is nearly always ordered?

---

[46] *Security First Corp. v. U.S. Die Casting & Dev. Co.*, 687 A.2d at 568.

Would you be in favor of a stricter standard? If so, what standard would you use?

   d. Justice Holland suggests that the standard might be changed if empirical evidence showed that shareholders' economic interest would be benefited from the change. Do you agree that the touchstone in determining the scope of shareholder inspection rights is shareholder economic benefit? Should that be the standard? Is that standard consistent with the history of shareholder inspection in Delaware? See casebook page 565.

Chapter 16
Shareholder Governance Questions Most Often Seen in the Privately Held Corporation

Page 600-601
Replace the formulas with the following:

Formula 1
To find the number of directors that can be elected with *s* shares:

$$D - INT\left(\frac{(S-s) \times (D+1)}{S}\right) = d$$

s = number of voting shares your faction controls
S = total number of voting shares
D = total number of director slots to be filled
d = the number of directors your faction can be certain of electing.

For those occasions when controlling more shares is possible, you can determine the number of shares necessary to elect a desired number of directors by using this formula:

Formula 2

$$INT\left(\frac{S \times d}{D+1}\right) + 1 = s$$

s = the number of voting shares your faction needs to elect "d" directors.

Finally, and often critically, one must know how many *votes* to give one's candidate(s) to ensure election. The formula is:

Formula 3

To find the number of votes, V, necessary to cast for each candidate to ensure that candidate's election:

$$\text{INT}\left(\frac{(S-s) \times D}{(D-d)+1}\right)+1 = V$$

V = the number of votes that must be cast per candidate to ensure election of "d" directors.

Chapter 19
Limited Liability Companies

Page 753
Add the following case before "*b. Managerial* ":

Puleo v. Topel
856 N.E.2d 1152 (Ill. App. 2006)

Presiding Justice QUINN delivered the opinion of the court:

Plaintiffs Philip Puleo, Malex Corporation, Amy Derksen, Chani Derus, Robert Filiczkowski, YSPEX, Inc., Jacob Lesgold, Van Ratsavongsay, and Bryan Weiss appeal the order of the circuit court dismissing their claims against defendant Michael Topel (Topel). On appeal, plaintiffs contend that the circuit court erred by finding that Topel could not be held personally liable for obligations incurred on behalf of defendant Thinktank, LLC (Thinktank), after the company was involuntary dissolved.

The record shows that effective May 30, 2002, Thinktank, a limited liability company (LLC) primarily involved in web design and web marketing, was involuntarily dissolved by the Illinois Secretary of State. The dissolution was due to Thinktank's failure to file its 2001 annual report as required by the Illinois Limited Liability Company Act (the Act) (805 ILCS 180/35-25(1) (West 2004)).

Thereafter, on December 2, 2002, plaintiffs, independent contractors hired by Topel, filed a complaint against Topel and Thinktank in which they alleged breach of contract, unjust enrichment, and claims under the account stated theory. Those claims stemmed from plaintiffs' contention that Topel, who plaintiffs alleged was the sole manager and owner of Thinktank, knew or should have known of Thinktank's involuntary dissolution, but nonetheless continued to conduct business as Thinktank from May 30, 2002, through the end of August 2002. They further contended that on or about August 30, 2002, Topel informed Thinktank employees and independent contractors, including plaintiffs, that the company was ceasing operations and that their services were no longer needed. Thinktank then failed to pay plaintiffs for work they had performed.

On or about April 4, 2003, Thinktank and Topel served their answer to the complaint on plaintiffs. In response, plaintiffs filed a motion for summary judgment on April 25, 2003. In that motion, plaintiffs argued that the only allegations that Thinktank and Topel denied in their answer pertained to Lesgold. As such, plaintiffs contended that there was no genuine issue of material fact and, thus, they were entitled to judgment as a matter of law. Subsequently, on June 6, 2003, plaintiffs filed a request to admit.

Although neither Thinktank nor Topel filed a response to plaintiffs' motion for summary judgment, they filed a response to plaintiffs' request to admit. Therein, defendants denied that Topel, as sole manager and owner of Thinktank, was in a position to know that Thinktank had been involuntarily dissolved by the Illinois Secretary of State or that the company was operating while dissolved during the period beginning on May 30, 2002.

On September 2, 2003, the circuit granted plaintiffs' motion for judgment on the pleadings against Thinktank. Thereafter, on October 16, 2003, plaintiffs filed a separate motion for summary judgment against Topel. [P]laintiffs contended that Topel, as a principal of Thinktank, an LLC, had a legal status similar to a shareholder or director of a corporation, who courts have found liable for a dissolved corporation's debts. Thus, plaintiffs argued that Topel was personally liable for Thinktank's debts. Topel did not file a response, and plaintiffs subsequently argued that Topel's failure to respond should be treated as a failure to contest their motion and that judgment should be entered for them.

On March 25, 2004, the circuit court denied plaintiffs' motion for summary judgment against Topel. Subsequently, plaintiffs filed a motion to reconsider on July 1, 2004, which the circuit court denied on August 23, 2004. In doing so, the circuit court acknowledged that Topel continued to do business as Thinktank after its dissolution and that the contractual obligations at issue were incurred after the dissolution. However, the court then stated:

> This court bases its decision on its reading of the Illinois Limited Liability Company Act. Specifically, this court reads 805 ILCS 180/10-10 in concert with 805 ILCS 180/35-7 as well as the legislative notes to 805 ILCS 180/10-10 to determine that the Illinois Legislature did not intend to hold a member of a Limited Liability Company liable for debts incurred after the Limited Liability Company had been involuntarily dissolved.

Finally, on January 6, 2005, the circuit court entered a final order dismissing all of plaintiffs' claims against Topel with prejudice. The court stated in pertinent part: "Based upon the Court's prior finding that the Illinois Legislature did not intend to hold a member of a Limited Liability Company liable for debts incurred after the Limited Liability Company had been involuntarily dissolved, the Court finds that all of Plaintiffs' claims against Defendant Topel within the Complaint fail as a matter of law, as they are premised upon Defendant Topel's alleged personal liability for obligations incurred in the name of Thinktank LLC after it had been involuntarily dissolved by the Illinois Secretary of State."

Plaintiffs now appeal that order.

We initially note that Topel has not filed a brief. Nonetheless, we may proceed under the principles set forth in *First Capitol Mortgage Corp. v. Talandis Construction Corp.,* 345 N.E.2d 493 (Ill. 1976).

In this court, plaintiffs contend that the circuit court erred in dismissing their claims against Topel. In making that argument, plaintiffs acknowledge that the issue as to whether a member or manager of an LLC may be held personally liable for obligations incurred by an involuntarily dissolved LLC appears to be one of first impression under the Act. That said, plaintiffs assert that it has long been the law in Illinois that an officer or director of a dissolved corporation has no authority to exercise corporate powers and, thus is personally liable for any debts he incurs on behalf of the corporation after its dissolution. Plaintiffs reason that Topel, as managing member of Thinktank, similarly should be held liable for debts the company incurred after its dissolution.

We first look to the provisions of the Act as they provided the trial court its basis for its ruling. When reviewing a statute, the cardinal rule is to ascertain and give effect to the intent of the legislature. The plain meaning of the language in the statute provides the best indication of legislative intent. Where the statutory language is clear, the court must give it effect without resorting to other aids for construction. Further, when a statute is amended, it is presumed that the legislature meant to change the law as it formerly existed.

As stated, the circuit court relied on sections 10-10 and 35-7 of the Act in making its ruling. Section 10-10 provides:

(a) Except as otherwise provided in subsection (d) of this Section, the debts, obligations, and liabilities of a limited liability company, whether arising in contract, tort, or otherwise, are solely the debts, obligations, and liabilities of the company. A member or manager is not personally liable for a debt, obligation, or liability of the company solely by reason of being or acting as a member or manager.

(b) (Blank)

(c) The failure of a limited liability company to observe the usual company formalities or requirements relating to the exercise of its company powers or management of its business is not a ground for imposing personal liability on the members or managers for liabilities of the company.

(d) All or specified members of a limited liability company are liable in their capacity as members for all or specified debts, obligations, or liabilities of the company if:

(1) a provision to that effect is contained in the articles of organization; and

(2) a member so liable has consented in writing to the adoption of the provision or to be bound by the provision. 805 ILCS 180/10-10 (West 2004).

Section 35-7 provides:

> (a) A limited liability company is bound by a member or manager's act after dissolution that:
> > (1) is appropriate for winding up the company's business; or
> > (2) would have bound the company under Section 13-5 before dissolution, if the other party to the transaction did not have notice of the dissolution.
>
> (b) A member or manager who, with knowledge of the dissolution, subjects a limited liability company to liability by an act that is not appropriate for winding up the company's business is liable to the company for any damage caused to the company arising from the liability. 805 ILCS 180/35-7 (West 2004).

Section 10-10 clearly indicates that a member or manager of an LLC is not personally liable for debts the company incurs unless each of the provisions in subsection (d) is met. In this case, plaintiffs cannot establish either of the provisions in subsection (d). They have not provided this court with Thinktank's articles of organization, much less a provision establishing Topel's personal liability, nor have they provided this court with Topel's written adoption of such a provision. As such, under the express language of the Act, plaintiffs cannot establish Topel's personal liability for debts that Thinktank incurred after its dissolution.

As plaintiffs contend, similar to the Business Corporation Act (BCA) (see 805 ILCS 5/12.30 (West 2004)), the Act explicitly provides that an LLC continues after dissolution only for the purpose of winding up its business (805 ILCS 180/35-3 (West 2004)). However, as plaintiffs concede in their brief, the Act does not contain a provision similar to section 3.20 of the Business Corporation Act, which provides:

> "All persons who assume to exercise corporate powers without authority so to do shall be jointly and severally liable for all debts and liabilities incurred or arising as a result thereof." 805 ILCS 5/3.20 (West 2004).

Moreover, we observe that section 35-7 of the Act explicitly provides that a member or manager of an LLC who, with knowledge of the dissolution, exceeds the scope of his authority during the wrapping up of a company's business is liable *to the company* for any damages arising from the liability. 805 ILCS 180/35-7(b) (West 2004). The Act, however, contains no language concerning a member or manager's liability to a third party. That silence speaks volumes when viewed in conjunction with the legislature's amendment of the former version of section 10-10.

Prior to its amendment, section 10-10 provided:

(a) A member of a limited liability company shall be personally liable for any act, debt, obligation, or liability of the limited liability company or another member or manager to the extent that a shareholder of an Illinois business corporation is liable in analogous circumstances under Illinois law.

(b) A manager of a limited liability company shall be personally liable for any act, debt, obligation, or liability of the limited liability company or another manager or member to the extent that a director of an Illinois business corporation is liable in analogous circumstances under Illinois law. 805 ILCS 180/10-10 (West 1996).

In 1998, however, the legislature amended section 10-10 and in doing so removed the above language which explicitly provided that a member or manager of an LLC could be held personally liable for his or her own actions or for the actions of the LLC to the same extent as a shareholder or director of a corporation could be held personally liable. As we have not found any legislative commentary regarding that amendment, we presume that by removing the noted statutory language, the legislature meant to shield a member or manager of an LLC from personal liability.

Nonetheless, plaintiffs ask this court to disregard the 1998 amendment and to imply a provision into the Act similar to section 3.20 of the Business Corporation Act. We cannot do so.

In the case at bar, we ... decline plaintiffs' request to ignore the statutory language. When the legislature amended section 10-10 (805 ILCS 180/10-10 (West 2004)), it clearly removed the provision that allowed a member or manager of an LLC to be held personally liable in the same manner as provided in section 3.20 of the Business Corporation Act. Thus, the Act does not provide for a member or manager's personal liability to a third party for an LLC's debts and liabilities, and no rule of construction authorizes this court to declare that the legislature did not mean what the plain language of the statute imports.

We, therefore, find that the circuit court did not err in concluding that the Act did not permit it to find Topel personally liable to plaintiffs for Thinktank's debts and liabilities. We agree with plaintiff that the circuit court's ruling does not provide an equitable result. However, the circuit court, like this court, was bound by the statutory language.

Accordingly, we affirm the judgment of the circuit court of Cook County.

Notes and Questions

1. Reality Check

a. How can Mr. Topel prevail if he didn't even file a brief?

b. Does the court use the same approach as in *New Horizons Supply Cooperative*?

c. What is the theory the plaintiffs use to try to hold Mr. Puleo personally liable?

d. Why did the court reject the plaintiffs' arguments?

2. Suppose

a. Imagine that Illinois had never adopted a statute addressing personal liability for LLC members or managers. Would the court's analysis or the result be different?

b. Imagine that Illinois enacted section 10-10 in its original version and never amended it. Would the court's analysis or the result be different?

c. Imagine that Illinois initially enacted section 10-10 in its current version (i.e., never adopted the original language) and never amended it. Would the court's analysis or the result be different?

d. Suppose this case arose in Wisconsin, as *New Horizons Supply Cooperative* did. Would the court's analysis or the result be different?

e. Suppose *New Horizon Supply Cooperative* arose in Illinois. Would the court's analysis or the result in that case be different?

4. What Do You Think?

a. Do you think that the Wisconsin statute in *New Horizon Supply Cooperative*, the original section 10-10, or the amended section 10-10 is the best statute? Do you think there is a better approach?

b. Do you agree with the inference the court drew from the legislature's amendment of the LLC liability statute? Are there other inferences that could be drawn from the amendment?

5. You Draft It

a. Draft a statute that reflects the appropriate rule regarding the personal liability of LLC members and managers. The text of the Wisconsin statute from *New Horizons Supply Cooperative*, the original version of Illinois section 10-10, and the amended version of Illinois section 10-10 are set out below.

Wisconsin 183.0304

Liability of members to 3rd parties.

(1) The debts, obligations and liabilities of a limited liability company, whether arising in contract, tort or otherwise, shall be solely the debts, obligations and liabilities of the limited liability company. [A] member or manager of a limited liability company is not personally liable for any debt, obligation or liability of the limited liability company, except that a member or manager may become personally liable by his or her acts or conduct other than as a member or manager.

(2) Notwithstanding sub. (1), nothing in this chapter shall preclude a court from ignoring the limited liability company entity under principles of common law of this state that are similar to those applicable to business corporations and shareholders in this state and under circumstances that are not inconsistent with the purposes of this chapter.

Illinois 805 ILCS 180/10-10 (original version)

(a) A member of a limited liability company shall be personally liable for any act, debt, obligation, or liability of the limited liability company or another member or manager to the extent that a shareholder of an Illinois business corporation is liable in analogous circumstances under Illinois law.

(b) A manager of a limited liability company shall be personally liable for any act, debt, obligation, or liability of the limited liability company or another manager or member to the extent that a director of an Illinois business corporation is liable in analogous circumstances under Illinois law.

Illinois 805 ILCS 180/10-10 (amended version)

(a) Except as otherwise provided in subsection (d) of this Section, the debts, obligations, and liabilities of a limited liability company, whether arising in contract, tort, or otherwise, are solely the debts, obligations, and liabilities of the company. A member or manager is not personally liable for a debt, obligation, or liability of the company solely by reason of being or acting as a member or manager.

(b) (Blank)

(c) The failure of a limited liability company to observe the usual company formalities or requirements relating to the exercise of its company powers or management of its business is not a ground for imposing personal liability on the members or managers for liabilities of the company.

(d) All or specified members of a limited liability company are liable in their capacity as members for all or specified debts, obligations, or liabilities of the company if:

(1) a provision to that effect is contained in the articles of organization; and

(2) a member so liable has consented in writing to the adoption of the provision or to be bound by the provision.